THIS IS REALLY HAPPENING

True Stories
by Erin Chack

RAZORBILL
An Imprint of Penguin Random House

RAZORBILL

An Imprint of Penguin Random House
Penguin.com

Copyright © 2017 Erin Chack

ISBN: 978-0-448-49358-9

Printed in the United States of America

1 3 5 7 9 10 8 6 4 2

Book design by Corina Lupp

For Sarge

CONTENTS

GIRL-SHAPED TORNADO

Cancer is hard. Obviously. Watching less than five minutes of any Lifetime Original Movie will tell you that. When I got cancer at the ripe young age of nineteen, I had seen the movies and thought I knew what to expect. Losing my hair? That was an obvious hard part. It felt a bit like that scene in *V for Vendetta* when Natalie Portman is shaking in a prison cell while her captor unceremoniously shaves off her long chestnut curls, except afterward I didn't look like Natalie Portman and I didn't get to blow up England.

Being very, very sick for months on end? Also obviously hard. At no point did I think that the nausea, the body aches, the mouth sores, the chills, the hemorrhoids, and the constant exhaustion wouldn't eventually take a toll on my mood.

But telling my friends I had cancer? That was a sneaky-hard part, one Lifetime didn't prepare me for. I guess I don't know what I expected would happen when I let the people closest to me know that I was about to transform into a naked mole rat but with a smaller chance of survival, but I hoped the script would go something like this:

ME: Hello, friend. I have the cancer.

THEM: Thank you for letting me know, friend. Let's go eat a pizza and resume our normal activities.

This, surprisingly, is not how it went. Telling someone you have cancer isn't like updating them on some fact about your life, like you've decided to go to grad school or you've stopped shaving your armpits. Telling someone you have cancer makes them feel bad. Really bad. Like, "Why would you do this specifically to me during my otherwise happy life?" bad. It's a delicate conversation, one that should be handled with care by a person who is good at it. I very quickly learned that, like dancing or knowing the right amount of spaghetti to cook, I was very, very not good at it.

When my parents called my boyfriend, Sean, and me into their bedroom to tell us the test results were back and I did, in fact, have cancer, I didn't freak out. I sort of already knew, since this was the third test, which was confirming the results of the first two tests, and I figured healthy people don't need triple-checking. Instead, I immediately turned to Sean and told him I'd need to borrow his Camry in the morning. He handed me the keys without saying a word.

The next day I drove fifty miles down the Garden State Parkway to a small New Jersey town where two of my closest college friends, Marly and Elena, lived. I wanted to tell my college friends first, figuring it would be the easiest. The initial lump discovery and subsequent tests had happened during the last few months of freshman year, so telling them I had cancer felt more like confirming a terrible suspicion than dropping a bomb.

How I attended a college four hours from my home and ended up making friends with two girls from Red Bank, New Jersey, is still one of the biggest mysteries of my life, but on that day I was grateful for the efficiency. Two birds, one tumorous stone. Marly met me at Elena's house, and the three of us sat on the front lawn ripping out fistfuls of grass while I told them, yeah, that lump was a lump, and yeah, I do have cancer. They hugged me from either side, and then we fell back onto the ground, looking up at the cloudless blue sky. It was a perfect May day.

"We have to call Olivia," I said. They both nodded, looking into the middle distance. Olivia was my roommate, and the fourth of our quartet, but she happened to live three hours in the opposite direction. With Marly and Elena at my side, I repeated my script to Olivia, this time over a crackly flip-phone speaker.

Since telling my college friends had gone relatively smoothly, I got overconfident about telling my home friends. But what I didn't account for was the fact that they had no idea something serious had been going on while I was away at college. My insistent Hey, can we meet up? text messages were taken as "I know we've only been home for a few days, but I've already rearranged my childhood bedroom thirteen times and I'm very bored, please hang out with me," which they brushed off. So with one of my best friends, Reid, I took a more aggressive route.

I'm coming over, I texted him. I shoved my phone in the front pocket of my jeans and dragged my purple Trek mountain bike out of the garage. I'd had the bike since fourth grade, and when I rode it I felt like a circus bear riding a tricycle, but without a car a circus bear I'd remain. Before I swung my leg over the too-low seat, I got a text back.

OK but hurry we're going out for Kirsten's birthday in an hour, he said. Kirsten was Reid's little sister and was turning fifteen that day. As I biked down the quiet suburban side streets, I wondered if telling Reid before a family dinner was a bad idea, but the wheels were quite literally already in motion. If I didn't tell him then, I was afraid I would lose my nerve and never get around to it. I imagined running into him at the bagel store in town completely bald and mumbling, "Oh yeah, I forgot to mention . . ."

When I got to Reid's house, I ditched my bike on his front lawn and knocked on the door. I heard his dog, Teddy, barking from somewhere deep in the house, then the tap-tap-tap of his doggy nails on the hardwood floor growing louder until he was barking so close to the door that the knocker rattled. Teddy was a big white-and-brown-spotted mutt with a reputation for being the dumbest, sweetest dog in town. He once knocked over and drank an entire can of beer at a party in Reid's basement when we were in high school. He was the drunkest one there.

"TEDDY!" Reid's mom, Chris, yelled. There was a clicking of locks and then the door swung open. She stood hunched over, trying to restrain an excited Teddy by his collar.

"Erin! Hi!" She threw her free arm around me in a half hug and patted my back. "Are you coming with us to Kirsten's birthday dinner?"

"Hi, Chris, hi, Teddy," I said as Teddy shoved his snout into my palm, sniffing for invisible treats. "Nope! Just gotta talk to Reid real quick." My heart suddenly began to race.

"He's upstairs, I think." She turned her head and yelled over her shoulder, "REID, ERIN'S HERE."

"OK, I'M UPSTAIRS," I heard him yell back.

She rolled her eyes and dragged Teddy out of the way so I could pass. I ran up the stairs and caught Kirsten coming out of the bathroom.

"Happy birthday, Keek!" I said, and I gave her a hug. She looked just like Reid: blond and blue-eyed with a cleft in her chin—the kind of kids that come in a brand-new picture frame before you replace the display with your own less attractive family.

"Hey! Thanks! Welcome home! Are you coming to dinner?" she asked.

"Nope, I can only stay for a minute," I said as I scooted past her to Reid's room.

I knocked on Reid's door and then entered without waiting for permission. He was bent over a suitcase on his bed, unpacking from school.

"He-e-ey," he said, tossing a shirt midfold back into his suitcase to greet me. "We did it! We survived freshman year!" He walked over to me with his arms spread and scooped me into a bear hug, leaning backward until my toes left the ground.

"Yeah, ha. Sophomores!" I said, once I was safely back on my feet. I wondered if I'd still be considered a sophomore if I never made it back to school.

"I've got a few days before lifeguarding picks up again. We should go hiking at Ramapo. Are you working at the pool this year?"

"I'm not," I said, taking a seat on the edge of his bed next to the suitcase. I felt nauseated. Everything was so normal—working at the pool, hiking at Ramapo—like this summer was a movie and someone had just un-paused it. And there I was, about to un-normal everything, a girl-shaped tornado in his bedroom.

"Oh yeah, I don't blame you. I quit Oradell. Got a job at Westwood instead. They have a snack stand, so it was an easy decision. Do you have anything else lined up for the summer?"

"Yeah, kinda," I said. A swell of adrenaline took over, and I realized this might be my only window. "Actually, hey, remember a few weeks ago when we were Skyping and you asked how things were and I said good but I had to get some weird medical tests done and you said, 'Hope everything goes OK'?"

"Yeah," he said, pulling out a bright-orange Virginia Tech T-shirt. He used his chin to pin the shirt to his chest as he folded the sleeves.

"Ha, yeah. So, everything didn't go OK," I said.

Reid let the shirt fall and crossed his arms. "OK," he said.

"OK, so." I swallowed a dry, hard swallow. "I have cancer?"

"You have what?"

"I, um, I have cancer. Hodgkin's lymphoma. I probably won't die, they said. Like, from this. I mean, I will one day. Everyone dies! Anyway, sorry."

Reid blinked a couple of times, and his face reddened. "You have cancer?"

"Yeah, but it's OK. Are you OK?"

He shoved his suitcase over and sat down next to me on the bed.

"No," he said.

"I'm sorry," I said again.

"Please don't say sorry for having cancer," he said, pushing the heels of his hands into his eyes.

"Sorry," I said. "I mean—shit."

Reid lay back on his bed. "Wha—what does this mean?"

"Cells are rapidly dividing—"

"No, I mean, like, do you have to start chemotherapy?"

"Yes," I said, lying down on the bed next to him.

"When?"

"The day after Memorial Day."

"That's this week."

"Yes."

We lay in silence staring up at the ceiling. I listened to our syncopated breaths and wondered what I was supposed to say next. Finally, I turned my head toward him. A tear rolled down the side of Reid's face and disappeared into the pattern of his bedspread.

"You don't have to cry," I said.

"I'm not doing it on purpose," he said.

"I know," I said. "I'm sorry."

"Stop saying sorry."

"So—sooo sore. I'm so sore from biking here."

"Shut up," Reid said, but he was laughing a little.

"OK," I said.

Reid crushed tears against the corners of his eyes while we lay there, until finally his mom called up the stairs.

"REEEID, KIIIRSTEN, IT'S TIME FOR DIIINER," she sang-yelled.

Reid took a deep breath. "OOOK," he yelled back down.

Together we stood up from the bed and then turned to face each other. He had stopped crying but his eyes were red and puffy. I threw my arms around his middle and squeezed.

He sighed and pressed his cheek on my forehead. "It's

going to be OK," he said. I wasn't sure if he was talking to me or himself.

"Yeah, totally, you're about to eat a delicious meal with the fam," I said. "What's better than that?"

He frowned. "You know what I mean."

Reid looked down at his shirt.

"OK, well. I gotta change," he said after a beat.

"It's cool, I'm gonna take off," I told him. "Text me if you need anything, I guess."

"Yeah. You, too," he said.

I left his room and shut the door behind me, pausing for a minute at the top of the stairs to let out a breath I didn't realize I had been holding. When I made it to the landing, Reid's dad, Mark, was walking by.

"Erin! You're home!" he said, grabbing me by the shoulders and pulling me into a hug. "Are you—"

"No, not coming to dinner. But thank you!"

"No, I was going to say 'alright.' You look . . . not like yourself."

"Oh," I said. "Yeah, I'm fine. Just gotta get home. See you!"

I left before he could say another word.

On the bike ride home I decided to stop at the woods near my old elementary school. It was late afternoon and the sun cast a warm yellow light on the tops of the trees. I hid my bike in a bush and followed a path to a stream where as a kid I used to flip rocks over looking for newts just so I could feel them wriggle in my hands for a minute before releasing them again. I walked along the stream until it fed into the ice-skating pond, long since thawed in the late spring weather, and sat on an old rusted metal bench.

Sitting in front of the pond I thought about the time when I was ten and I made my neighbor Little Erin (she was two years my junior but we were the same exact height) take a pit stop there as we were walking home from school together. It was an unseasonably warm winter day, but a slick layer of ice still covered the surface. The NO SKATING sign hung from the pole, squeaking in the breeze, but I told Little Erin I was going to see how far I could walk on the surface. She stayed near the edge while I moved toward the middle of the pond taking light, sure steps until—*crack*—the ice broke and my leg shot through. In that instant I was absolutely sure that I would get trapped under the ice, banging my fists against the frozen surface while the cold slowly took me. When I snapped back to reality, I realized I was standing in water no deeper than my ten-year-old knees. It was more of a marsh, really: a foot of mud with a couple of inches of ice water on top.

Up until now, that was probably the closest I'd ever come to death.

Back at my house I called Sean from the landline phone.

"Hey," he said. "How'd it go?"

"Not so good," I said. "I might've ruined Kirsten's fifteenth birthday."

"That bad, eh?"

"Wait," I said. "Reid just texted me. It says, 'I'm currently crying in the bathroom at Pancho's Burritos.' Fuck, man."

"Oh wow. Yeah, I guess that's a thing that's gonna happen."

"I can't do it again. It's too shitty. I can't keep, like, bumming people out."

"Yeah, maybe we gotta try being more casual about it. Maybe if we tell people in a way that's not intense they won't have intense reactions."

"I'm down to try it," I said. "I'm down to try anything."

We tried it on our friend Joe first. Sean had met Joe through skateboarding, and I had met Joe through Sean. He lived a town over and only hit us up either to skate or eat fast food. It was a simple relationship. You knew exactly what you were getting when Joe called.

And one day, before Memorial Day, Joe called. I was sitting on Sean's bed flipping through an issue of *Thrasher*, and Sean was watching videos on his computer when his phone buzzed. He flipped it open without taking his eyes from the screen.

"Hey, Joe," he said. "I'm just hanging at home—Yeah, she's here—What's up with you?—Oh, Tuesday?" Sean looked at me. "Uh, one sec." He covered the mouthpiece with his palm. "Hey," he whispered to me. "I'm gonna do it." He shook the phone to indicate what he meant. I nodded.

"Actually, uh, Joe, I can't skate Tuesday. I have to go with Erin to the hospital because she has cancer." Sean looked at me wide-eyed and shrugged. I shrugged back. "OK— Sure— OK, bye."

He hung up.

"What'd he say?" I asked, amazed at how quickly the conversation had ended.

"He said, 'OK, cool,' then he asked if we wanted to go to KFC."

We stared at each other for a moment across the room. And then we burst into laughter at the exact same time.

"WHAT?" I said.

"I swear!" he said.

"OH my god," I said. "That couldn't have been more

casual. It's like you told him I had a dentist appointment."

"I know. Insane!"

"Classic Joe," I said.

Sean shook his head. "I told you: If we are cool about it, people will be cool about it."

We met Joe at KFC an hour later. Before leaving Sean's house, I made myself a peanut butter and jelly sandwich because I was on strict dietary restrictions from my oncologist: no fast food, no salad bars, no fruit without a peel, no sushi, no steak tartare—basically no foods that could risk giving me an infection. I still looked forward to hanging out at KFC despite not being allowed to eat anything. Hanging out at fast-food restaurants was what we normally did, and I wanted more than anything for everything to remain normal.

At KFC Joe and Sean ordered a pile of food and I got a bottle of water. Once they had their trays, we picked a booth at the back of the restaurant and settled in. Suddenly I found myself in a flurry of paper wrappers, cardboard boxes, and the intoxicating smells of greasy potato and meat products. My eyelids fluttered.

"Sucks you guys can't make it Tuesday," Joe said. "We're driving down to Sayreville to skate the park and then going to the beach after."

"Yeah, next time," Sean said.

"Yeah," said Joe. He was pushing potato wedges into his mouth two at a time. I could hear the crispy fried skin crunching with every bite. Suddenly the PB&J in my stomach seemed very lonely.

"Oh my god, those wedges look so good," I said, my mouth watering.

"Have one," Joe said, sliding the container over to me.

"I wish," I said. "But I probably shouldn't."

"Why? Are you on a diet?"

"Yeah, well, the doctors said to avoid fast food so I'm trying to be good about it."

"Doctors?" Joe's eyes flicked between Sean and me. "You sick or something?"

Sean and I looked at each other, brows furrowed.

"Joe," I said, turning to him slowly. "I have cancer. Sean told you on the phone."

"THAT'S WHAT YOU SAID?!" A little piece of potato tumbled out of Joe's gaping mouth and landed on the tray.

"Yeah, dude. What'd you think I said?"

"I don't know! I kinda stopped listening after you said you couldn't skate! You said it so casually I assumed it wasn't important." Joe sank his head into his greasy hands. "Oh my god, this is terrible."

"It's OK, I'll be OK," I said. For a moment I felt like I had been transported back to Reid's bedroom. *Please don't cry,* I thought. *Please, please, please.*

"No, I mean"—Joe looked at me through his splayed fingers—"I can't believe I found out you have cancer in a fucking KFC."

I stopped telling people after that. They got upset when I was serious and they got upset when I was casual. It seemed like the only way not to upset anyone was to avoid the subject completely. And that strategy worked for a little while. But then, like with all forms of procrastination, time caught up with me.

I had my first chemotherapy treatment, then my second, then sometime around the third or the fourth my hair started falling out in clumps. Eventually I shaved my head. My oncologist wrote me a prescription for a wig that I never filled. For me the idea of wearing a wig felt like someone telling me, "You are very sick, but try not to look like it." I did, however, wear beanies and hoods, a mid-June look that probably drew as much attention to me as my shiny, bald head would have.

It was around this time that our friend Jordan, another skate friend turned friend-friend, called Sean to hang out one night. Sean and I realized that Jordan had somehow slipped into the pile of people who didn't yet know I was sick. We figured he wouldn't take the news too hard since Jordan and I were new friends and he was deeply committed to not caring about anything. Still, we reasoned that showing up to his house completely bald could make the needle on his Fuck-O-Meter jump from "Not Giving One" to "What the—?"

During the car ride to Jordan's house, Sean and I tried to put together a game plan.

"Should we tell him right away?" I asked.

"No," Sean said, gripping the steering wheel and keeping his eyes on the road. "I think we should wait for an opportunity after we've settled in."

"You don't think that's weird? To be hanging out with someone for an hour or two and then get told, hey, I have some incredibly serious news?"

"I'm not saying it's flawless. I just think it's better than showing up at his house with awful news and then expecting to hang out like everything's normal after."

"But what if there's never a good moment?" I asked.

"I don't know," Sean said. "Let's just hope there is."

We were both quiet for a minute or two after that. As Sean merged onto Route 4, I wondered why I was even going over to Jordan's in the first place. My treatments were only supposed to last six months, and it would probably only take a month or two after that for my hair to start growing back. Maybe I could just avoid him for the better part of a year. Sure, he was one of my favorite people, the kind of guy who could make you laugh so hard in the vegetable aisle of a grocery store that you had to sit on the floor to stop yourself from peeing. But in that moment cutting him out of my life seemed less painful than having to tell him.

Before I knew it we were in Jordan's bedroom watching bad TV. Jordan was lying on the floor on his side propped up on his elbow and flipping through channels while Sean and I sat on the edge of his bed. I was wearing my beanie and a sweatshirt with the hood up to hide my baldness, but after being inside for a while I felt a little river of sweat snake its way down the back of my neck. I tugged at the hood.

"There's. Nothing. To. Watch. Ever," Jordan said, switching the channel with each word. "I swear, television is like one giant contest to see who can make the worst show."

"Should we go somewhere?" Sean asked.

"I'm down," I said, imagining the crisp night air cooling my skin.

"Go where? There's nothing to do ever," Jordan said, looking at us over his shoulder.

I knew he was right. We were teenagers in suburban New Jersey. There were a finite number of fast-food restaurants, and we'd hung out at every one of them.

Jordan kept flipping. "Being alive is so boring," he said to no one. Then finally he found some clip show where a comedian reviews Internet videos and asked, "How's this?"

"Yeah," Sean said. "Fine."

"I don't care," I said.

Jordan put the remote down. "Thank Satan," he whispered to himself.

As if on cue, the show cut to commercial. Jordan let out a long, sad, "Nooooooo." He rolled onto his stomach with his face mashed in the navy carpeting. I sighed. This night was going nowhere.

Just then I felt something hitting my thigh. I looked down. Sean was patting my leg with one hand and pointing at the TV with the other. On the screen was a commercial for St. Jude's Children's Hospital. Little bald-headed children were smiling at the camera from their hospital beds. I looked at Sean. He nodded at me in slow motion, his eyes crazed. "This. Is. It," he mouthed.

Before I could object, Sean was clearing his throat.

"Uh, hey, Jordan," Sean said.

"What?" Jordan said without lifting his head from the carpet.

I wondered where Sean was going with this. He was a terrible improviser. I held my breath.

"Aren't bald kids *sooo* weird looking?" he asked.

Jordan's head snapped up. He looked at the TV, at the adorable children on screen, and then turned to Sean with a face twisted in absolute disgust.

"What. The fuck. Is *wrong* with you, man?"

It doesn't happen often, but there are times Sean and I are so in sync it's like I can hear his thoughts inside my own brain. This was one of those few and precious times. I knew exactly what to do next.

"Jordan," I said.

I waited for him to look at me and then, very slowly and without breaking eye contact, reached up and peeled back my beanie and hood, revealing my own shiny, bald head.

Jordan's face melted from disgust to absolute horror.

"What the FUCK?" he screamed. He rolled onto his side and clutched his knees to his chest. "You guys are *sick!*"

Sean and I roared with laughter until we were doubled over and slipping off the bed. Sean rolled onto his stomach and pounded the floor with his fist. I lay on my back and wallowed in the rare but beautiful pain of laughing so hard it hurts. I could feel the fibers of the carpet itching the skin on the back of my bald head.

"WHY WOULD YOU DO THIS?" Jordan yelled over our laughter, as if we had been planning this prank for weeks and had called St. Jude's to play a commercial on a station we might be watching on a random Wednesday night. He was still curled up in the fetal position, looking at us with huge, horrified eyes. "I can't believe you shaved your head to make a fucking *joke*!"

"Jordan!" I said, trying to catch my breath. "It's not a joke. I have cancer!" I could barely get the words out.

"It's true," Sean said, wiping tears from his eyes. "She does. We didn't know how to tell you."

Jordan uncurled his knees from his chest. He sat up and looked at us. "Wait, seriously?"

I felt the laughter get sucked out of my chest. "Yeah," I said, still lying on my back. "Seriously." Suddenly I missed the pain in my stomach.

"Whoa," Jordan said. "I don't know what to say. I'm sorry."

"Pretty sure we're the ones who should say sorry," I said, sitting up.

"Are you going to be alright?" Jordan said.

"I think so," I said. "I had a few treatments already."

"How are they?" he asked.

"Fucking terrible," I said.

"Fuck," said Jordan.

Some splashy music played from the TV, signaling the show had returned. Jordan looked over his shoulder at it.

"Do you want me to turn this off?" he asked.

"No," I said. "It's OK."

The three of us turned toward the TV, but no one could really pay attention after that.

I had another treatment later that week, and, like the treatments before, it completely laid me out. It felt like I had been hit by a truck, only while the truck was rolling over me it also gave me the flu. My muscles and joints ached. The inside of my mouth burned. I was tired and restless, sweating and cold. I felt like a prisoner of my own sick body.

Three days after the treatment I still felt horrible, which was around the time I normally would start to feel the life creep back into my toes. It was on that third day I got a call from my high school friend Dana. She wanted to know if I was interested in grabbing lunch at the deli between our houses, our ritual dating back to elementary school. In an effort to not give into how bad I felt, I told her sure, as long as she picked up a sandwich for me and brought it to my house. I'd pay her back, I told her. She agreed, so I rolled out of bed and pulled on my new uniform, a beanie and hoodie. Dana didn't know I was sick, and, as I waited for her to arrive, I decided I wasn't going to tell her. I didn't have the strength.

When Dana got to my house, she didn't comment on my appearance, probably figuring the beanie-hoodie look was something I'd picked up at college. We sat at my kitchen table and unwrapped our sandwiches: chicken cutlet on a round roll with lettuce, tomato, and mayo—the same order since sixth grade. Dana dug into hers, but I could only pick at the bread on mine. Chewing hurt. Everything hurt. And as the moments passed I became increasingly exhausted by having to pretend I felt fine.

"So school was good?" Dana asked as she poured herself a glass of iced tea from the fridge.

"Yeah," I said, resting my head in my hands. "Yeah, all good. You?"

"Really good! I think I'm going to apply to be an RA next year. You know, free room and board. Plus you get to live in a single, so."

"Yeah," I said. "Totally. Single."

I wanted to tell her that she'd be great at it, that her upbringing as an only child had given her a low tolerance for

bullshit and a high dose of self-respect, both essential quali-
ties in an RA. But instead I yanked the cords of my hoodie
tighter around my face and struggled to keep my eyes open.

Finally, I excused myself to use the bathroom. Once
I'd lowered myself onto the toilet, I peed with my head
resting on the sink. I sat there much longer than I needed to,
trying to gather up the energy to get up. I pulled my pants
up, washed my hands in slow motion, and shuffled into
the hallway. Before turning toward the kitchen, I caught
a glance of my parents' bedroom and spotted the bed,
perfectly made and glowing in a shaft of midday sunlight.
The fluffy stack of pillows was calling my name. *It wouldn't
hurt to lie down for a minute*, I thought. I turned away from
the kitchen where Dana was still eating, walked down the
hall to my parents' bed, and lay facedown in blankets that
smelled like my mom's shampoo.

One minute turned into five, and five turned into ten.
Soon, I lost track of how many minutes had passed. As
I faded in and out of sleep, I vaguely wondered if Dana
thought I was having sandwich-induced stomach issues,
but I also didn't care. I was too tired to care, or to do anything other than lie very still. Then I heard my mom, who
had been putzing around the house, come into her bedroom.
She let out a tiny gasp, surprised to see a body in her bed,

and I thought for a second she might yell at me for leaving my friend alone in the kitchen. Instead she pulled the comforter over me and drew the curtains. It made me feel both very old and very young, all at once.

I heard my mom walk down the hallway, into the kitchen. I heard her greet Dana and ask if she knew what was going on with me. Then, as I drifted off to sleep, I heard her calmly do the thing I had messed up so many times.

BURY ME WITH POISON IVY

My boyfriend, Sean, and I have been dating for so long that I remember when he only had three chest hairs. We met when I was fourteen years old in the aftermath of an early season hurricane—Ivan or Irene or Isabella or something. The storm had knocked out power throughout the county, flooding roads and basements and suspending school indefinitely. I had spent the morning at my friend Katie's house playing every board game we could find by candlelight until we got so bored that we decided to cast off into the wind-torn world.

Katie and I walked down the middle of wet-black streets, stepping over coiled wires and leap-frogging over the trunks of trees. The sky hung heavy and gray and everywhere around us was quiet, except for the occasional wail of a fire truck. Before long we found ourselves at the town park, a place we returned to again and again like teenage moths drawn to a very boring flame.

When we arrived, Katie recognized some friends from her high school huddled around a picnic table, three boys who looked old enough to have started families in other states. This was one of the perks of our friendship: Katie was two grades ahead of me so sometimes I got to meet high school boys, which in theory was the single coolest thing a middle school girl could ever hope for but, in practice, always made my insides turn to liquid. As much as I bragged about it to my friends, meeting high school boys terrified me. Today was no exception.

Katie tugged at my sleeve.

"Let's go say hi," she said.

Before I knew it I was facing a semicircle of man-boys as Katie introduced them one by one.

"Erin, this is Tomita, Dave, and Sean," she said, pointing at each of them.

"Hi," I said to the ground.

"Hi," they said back in unison.

We sat around the table talking about nothing, and I pretended to be interested in my thumbnail. I snuck a few looks at the boy named Sean, who seemed the most interesting based on the sole fact that he said the fewest amount of words. The problem was that I couldn't look directly at anyone who wasn't Katie, so instead of getting acquainted with Sean's light-brown eyes and the freckle on his bottom lip—features I would one day know better than my own—I picked away at my bloodied cuticle.

Eventually, Sean excused himself from the group and crossed the basketball courts to talk to a kid who was skateboarding alone, whom I recognized as someone in my grade named Terrence. We sat near each other in art class.

"Why is Sean talking to Terrence?" I asked Katie. I assumed our friendship was the only one on earth of its kind to bridge the chasm between middle school and high school.

"I think they skate together," Katie said.

Interesting, I thought. I had always liked Terrence. Sometimes during art class we'd switch shoes: my pristine Vans for his much cooler torn-up ones. (I was an entire foot taller than him and, due to the physics of eighth grade, the same shoe size.) If Sean got along with Terrence, and I got along with Terrence, maybe Sean and I would get along, too.

While the rest of the group chattered on, I watched Sean and Terrence. I loved how at ease Sean seemed, like he wasn't embarrassed to be caught talking to a middle schooler in broad daylight. He smiled a lot and kept his arms crossed over his chest in a way that commanded an authority I couldn't place. Then he said goodbye and shook Terrence's hand. I was mesmerized. The only people I knew of who shook hands were lawyers on TV.

Days later I badgered Katie for Sean's AIM screen name. I would never chat him for fear I'd self-combust, but I wanted to keep my eye on him (and maybe the relationship category of his profile, which, to my agony, I would soon discover was left cryptically blank). Finally, she relented, and I added his name to my buddy list: c1sk8r29. I never dared to click it, but my heart would race whenever I saw his name jump into the "Online" category. Then one day I got a message.

c1sk8r29: katie said u wanted 2 talk 2 me

My heart beat so hard I felt it in my shoes.

I owe so much to poison ivy. A few months after I met Sean in the park, he contracted a pretty bad case of it when his skateboard rolled into a bush of shiny green leaves. Days later, weeping sores covered the skin on his face and hands.

```
c1sk8r29: and my penis
c1sk8r29: because i didn't realize the oils
were on my hand when i went 2 pee
```

I was relieved to see Sean's messages pop up since our chats of late had gone from every other day to once a week if I was lucky. He was busy finishing up his sophmore year with finals and parties, and I was busy acting consciously aloof (I assumed that to a high school boy the only thing less appealing than a middle school girl is a middle school girl who chats first). Still, my stomach would do a backflip whenever his message box popped up on my screen, his standard "hey sup" in maroon Comic Sans.

But then summer vacation happened and everything changed. He was no longer busy, and I was no longer a middle schooler, since I'd be starting high school in the fall. And by some grace of the gods of teenage romance, Sean was covered in hideous rashes that couldn't be touched by daylight, which left him with nothing better to do than chat me all day long.

I, on the other hand, did have better things to do, but canceled them all to spend more screen time with him. Especially if it meant getting to hear more about his pus-covered weiner. The truth was, I was relieved to have an excuse to stay holed up in my dining room on the family PC for a week. I had recently broken up with a kid in my grade after a six-week stint of meeting up at the park to hold hands and closed-mouth kiss. He was dull, and I knew it even then—he insisted on being called by his last name (what were we, teammates?). But days after the breakup I saw a girl standing on the pegs on the back of his BMX bike as they cruised down Kinderkamack Road, and it ripped me in half. It was the first time I had felt any significant emotion for the boy, but I didn't mind the opportunity to avoid accidentally feeling it again. So Sean's oozing blisters and my bruised heart healed together, separately, across the Internet.

I don't remember much of what Sean and I talked about that week he was stuck indoors, just that we talked, and that it was the best seven days of my entire summer. At one point I told Sean that my cousin who lives in the Midwest had started dating a bull rider.

emu16: isnt that funny? bull riding in the midwest is like skateboarding here i guess

I didn't think much of it until a few hours later, when I absentmindedly checked his profile and saw that under

"Occupation" he had written "I am a bull rider." Maybe he liked the skateboarding analogy or maybe he blatantly misunderstood what I had meant. I didn't care, because either way it meant that I had made an impression on him, that our conversations lingered in his mind, that he thought about me.

When I die, cover my casket in wreaths of poison ivy.

The poison ivy week set a sort of precedent for our relationship, if you can call it that. After Sean's blisters turned to scabs, we both emerged pale and blinking from our respective computer rooms to return to the outside world. There was still a lot of summer to catch up on, but some mornings before biking to the town pool (me) and skateboarding in driveways (him) we'd catch each other online and—*bi-bing*—race to chat each other first. We'd talk about our upcoming days and what we had been up to since the last time we chatted. Our conversations were continuous and easy, unraveling like a thread on a sweater that could cover the moon.

I learned a lot about Sean. He had a sister and a single mom. He had moved to the neighboring town at the beginning of the year and he liked it so far. He thought high school was fine, a step up from the school in his old town. He was good at math but bad at Spanish. His favorite color

was green. He had a summer job at the carousel outside the
Van Suan Zoo selling tickets and cotton candy. He told me I
should never eat that cotton candy.

> **emu16:** why? whats wrong with it??
>
> **c1sk8r29:** nothins wrong w it but it has milk
> in it. ur lactose intolerant right?
>
> **emu16:** yeah . . .
>
> **emu16:** im pretty sure its just sugar tho?
>
> **c1sk8r29:** oh.
>
> **c1sk8r29:** rly??
>
> **c1sk8r29:** the thing it comes in looks like a
> milk carton. i just assumed that meant it had milk
> in it

I thought about that for days.

The best part of our conversations was that everything
was filtered through a computer screen. I felt safe there,
behind the glass. But then one day Sean invited me to hang
out with a couple of his friends in the park—perhaps a small
gesture of thanks after I kept him virtual company when he
was stuck home for a week.

I tried to play it like hanging out with upperclass-
men who weren't Katie was a totally normal thing for
me, but I remember the strange way my legs shook as

I walked to meet him. When I got to the park, I waved hello and then sat on the bleachers and ignored him, too scared to talk face-to-face. He waved back and continued skating around in circles, ollying a garbage can lid on the basketball courts with some kids I recognized from town but had never met. I pretended not to notice that Sean didn't notice I was ignoring him and talked to a girl named Jenna who was a grade ahead of me. I didn't know her well but people always said we looked alike: tall and spindly with brownish-blondish hair past our shoulders. Her older brother was in Sean's grade and was one of his best friends, so I figured that Sean probably spent a lot of time at their house. At her house. I found myself wondering if he thought she was pretty, because that would mean he thought I was pretty.

As we watched the boys roll around the basketball court, Jenna told me she could never skateboard. She said she would break records for the amount of cuts and bruises she'd receive—a self-inflicted lingchi. I nodded along, "same"-ing her to death, although I secretly wanted to try it, alone and away from an audience. It seemed fun—liberating, almost— and definitely a better way to spend an afternoon than sitting on the bleachers.

Jenna went on and on about her lifelong commitment

to being Bad at Sports. Soon the topic of scars came up. After we had rolled up every sleeve and pant leg to expose our own, Jenna called Sean over. My pulse drummed against my ears as he skated up to us, the summer sun a halo around his curly black hair.

"Hey, Sean, you got any scars?" she asked.

Sean pushed up his T-shirt sleeves and exposed the back of his arms, reaching back like he was scratching identical itches on his shoulder blades. Five-inch-long slashes of taut, puckered skin ran along his triceps.

"I accidentally punched my arms through a glass door when I was seven," Sean said. "I heard the ice-cream truck outside and couldn't wait. Saw my muscle on this one."

He leaned forward so we could inspect the thicker of the two scars. A wave of his scent—a mix of some hyper-masculine deodorant brand and fresh sweat—teased my nose as I squinted at the raised red skin. Slowly I reached up and with one finger traced the length of the scar from his elbow to his armpit, feeling the bumps of the ruined flesh. I felt an electric current shoot down my arm. It was the first time we had ever touched.

"DON'T TOUCH HIM," a voice yelled, and I jumped, pulling my hand back as if I had accidentally brushed against a hot stove.

One of Sean's friends was laughing at his own comedic timing.

"What do you want, to get pregnant?" he said through giggles.

Eventually the sun set on summer vacation and high school started the first week of September, which gave our relationship its first official label: schoolmates. I felt dumb and small wandering around the hallways on my first day, a tiny minnow swimming upstream in a river of overgrown salmon. I barely recognized anybody. Boys had dark prickly patches of facial hair, and girls twirled their car keys around their fingers. The chorus of voices all around me was an entire octave lower than in middle school. I clutched the straps of my giant backpack and hoped I wouldn't get swept away by a gust of teenage hormones. With the help of another minnow, a boy I had been friends with since elementary school, I found my locker on the second floor. I opened and closed it twice, realizing I had nothing to put in it. There was still time before my first class started, but I didn't want to risk looking like I was looking for someone to talk to, so I went downstairs to wait outside my first classroom.

I hadn't even reached the final step of the stairwell

when I saw Sean standing outside the main office, looking over his class schedule. Before I realized what I was doing I called his name. Sean looked up and smiled. His hair was damp, making it blacker and curlier than usual, and hung in his eyes. He must have showered only minutes before. I had been showered and dressed for almost two hours at that point. Oh, to be a junior.

"He-e-e-y," he said back. Sean walked over and pulled me into a hug. His wet hair squelched against my ear.

"Happy first day of high school," he said when we broke apart. The piney smell of his bar soap lingered between us.

"Is it happy?" I said. "I feel nothing but dread."

He laughed. "You'll get used to that."

I was about to reply when a group of my freshmen friends squealed my name as if we hadn't seen each other in decades. Nothing makes people nostalgic for friends they had hung out with earlier that week quite like the first day of school.

"I've gotta run," I said as the group thundered toward me.

"I'll look for you at lunch," Sean said.

"OK," I said, right as I was tackled by a group hug that dragged me down the hall. I watched Sean wave goodbye as he got smaller and smaller in my field of vision until he was swallowed up by a group of his own friends.

After the hugs and the I-can't-believe-we're-high-schoolers subsided, my friend Meg asked, "Wait, who was that you were talking to?"

"Oh," I said, feeling the skin on my stomach start to sweat. "Just a friend."

Our second official label.

But the first day of high school is the peak of high school, I soon learned. And I hated high school, which was just as bad as middle school, except with harder classes and more people to embarrass myself in front of. When I think of freshman year, it's through a fog of exhaustion and anxiety. School started too early. The halls were too crowded. The classes were too long.

There were so, so many rules about where I was allowed to be and at what time. I was a compulsively good student, but the stress of keeping my grades up ate away at me until I started having panic attacks so violent it felt like I was leaving my body and watching myself drown from across the room. When I finally got to leave the physical confines of school at the end of the day, I went home to mountains of homework. On the weekends, there were projects and reading assignments and studying. There was *always* studying.

That whole year I felt like someone was holding my nostrils to the surface of a murky pond and I could only breathe when I concentrated very hard. One false move and my lungs would fill with water.

The only way I survived freshman year was by looking forward to my brief and stilted interactions with Sean. High school didn't seem to get to him like it did me. He was an average student and never tried to be anything more than that. I, on the other hand, was constantly afraid that one bad grade would end my chances of going to a brand-name college. He had a reputation for being the Nicest Guy in eleventh grade, which made it seem like every single junior was his best friend, and on top of that he had his out-of-town skate crew to fall back on. Meanwhile, my friend group was suddenly in flux. My tightknit middle school group had dissolved, and I always seemed to be hanging with people who didn't quite get my jokes.

One time in gym class, I was playing indoor kickball with the other freshmen, and Michael Buchholz, the world's most enthusiastic kickball player, line-drived the ball straight at my head. The problem was that I had just finished yawning and when I opened my eyes I only had enough time to block my face. I managed to stop the ball with my hands, but the force knocked me backward until I found myself sitting on the ground in an *L*. It was almost as if my body decided to sit that play out without my consent. Reid ran over covering his mouth with one hand to conceal his laughter and extending the other to help me up while Buchholz stomped around the bases with his mascot-sized feet. I kept my head down even after I regained my composure. Earlier I had seen Sean on the other side of the gym playing basketball with the juniors. I didn't dare to check if he saw. But at the end of P.E. he jogged over to me, and I knew what was coming.

"Great reflexes before. I saw Buchholz tried to take you out," he said.

"Yeah, ha," I said, suddenly wishing the ball had literally killed me. "I didn't catch it though."

"Who cares? It looked like something out of *The Matrix*."

"Too bad there are no points for that," I said.

"There are in my book." He shrugged.

Only Sean could make getting smashed in the face with a kickball seem like a victory. His general chillness was a rock I could cling to while the waves of high school thrashed me, so that's exactly what I did.

Over the weeks I learned which hallways to walk down to catch a glimpse of Sean's face amid the hundreds of students pushing their way to class. I knew where he tended to sit at lunch and purposely tossed my crumpled brown bags into the garbage can by his table. After school, I took long, roundabout routes to pass by his locker. A simple wave, a smile, a "How was class?" was enough to make the constant grinding toil of high school life bearable. And then a few hours would go by and I would crave interacting with him again, like a smoker always reaching for her pack.

But then there was another girl. Alex.

One day after gym class, I overheard two junior girls in the locker room saying that Sean was thinking of asking Alex to the junior prom.

I felt sick as I pulled my sweaty T-shirt over my head, but a part of me knew it made sense. I was a freshman, a child. Alex was a junior. Why would a junior boy bring a freshman girl to his prom when he could bring an Alex? Sure, we were friends. But any acts of kindness he showed me were probably just that: kindness. After all, Sean was known for being incredibly, painfully nice, and I had probably misinterpreted his kindness as romantic feelings. Plus, Alex was adorable. Short and petite and olive skinned—my exact opposite. Sean and Alex would look great in a prom photo together with her corsage matching his boutonniere, their fingers intertwined on her hip.

And I would be home that night, watching a *SpongeBob SquarePants* marathon.

To preserve what little dignity I thought I had left, I went on the offensive. I chatted Sean one night after school, like I did most nights.

emu16: so . . .

emu16: junior proms in january, right? god what a nightmare. dresses and dancing and ugh

c1sk8r29: oh . . . yeah pretty wack i guess

emu16: yeah glad i have a couple of years before i have to deal with that shit

c1sk8r29: haha lucky u

The truth was I really *didn't* want to go to prom—dancing and dresses really were two of my least favorite things, not to mention the pressure of being his Date with a capital *D* when we weren't evening dating with a lower-case *d*—but I didn't want him to go without me either. As much as it pained me, I knew my only option was to remove myself from the situation entirely. He couldn't pass me up if I wasn't waiting in line. And if Alex and Sean started dating after prom, at least I wouldn't look like the sad freshman that thought she actually had a chance with the nice older guy.

A few days later, I was tying my sneakers on the bench in the locker room when I overheard that Sean had asked Alex to prom. I heard he did it in the school library during their study hall. I heard she squealed and hugged him and asked if he was serious no fewer than four times. And over the next few weeks I wished I could stop hearing things, that earwax would build up in my ear canal until all I could hear was the loud whooshing of my own breathing.

Eventually I heard that on the night of prom Sean and his friends went to Alex's mansion to take pre-prom photos. I heard Alex came down the spiral staircase, perfect dress perfect hair perfect makeup, like out of a John Hughes movie. I heard during the last slow dance of the night she tried to kiss him but he pulled his face away, and her lips landed on his chin.

I heard that he broke her heart that night because he had to tell her he liked someone else.

Things were weird between us after that. I think Sean felt bad for leading on a girl that liked him a lot, and I felt bad just existing as a human in this world. I wasn't sure what to do with all the rumors, or if there was even anything to do. I remember catching him near the vending machines during our lunch period not long after the promisode.

"Hey," he said.

"Hi."

We stood there in silence, bopping our heads to music that didn't exist. I wanted to ask how prom was, but I already knew, everyone knew, and I was sure if we talked about it he would be able to detect how many nights I spent wondering if I was the reason he turned his face away.

Instead I said, "You've got a hole in your jeans," and pointed to a spot just below his right front pocket.

"Yeah," he said, reaching down and tugging at the fabric of his boxers through the rip in his jeans as if to prove it was, in fact, a hole. They were blue and patterned with tiny orange basketballs.

"Do you . . . like basketball?" I asked.

He looked down at his boxers. "Oh," he said as he shook his head. "Not really."

"Oh," I said. "Me neither. I fell asleep at a Nets-Bulls game when I was six. Jordan was playing."

"Oh, no way," he said.

"Yeah," I said.

The head bopping started up again. "Well, see you around."

"See you around."

After we had a few more of these interactions, I was sure that I had blown it with Sean. Prom had been my big chance to tell him how I felt, and by saying I hated prom I had basically said I hated him. And maybe he liked a million girls, or maybe he didn't like any. Maybe he just didn't want to be kissed by Alex, the tiny, perfect olive, and maybe that had no bearing on how he felt about me, the non-tiny, non-perfect peeled banana.

Weeks passed. School got harder because talking to Sean got harder. It didn't help that it was February, the bleakest month of the year. Outside, the snow piles had crusted into ice piles, the cold somehow making cold things colder.

Then one day in first period, I decided enough was enough. I had missed my opportunity to be his Date and his date, but I could still preserve the friendship, what little of it remained. I resolved to talk to Sean at lunch, like the old days before prom ruined everything. So I spent second period drawing up a conversation topic to minimize any there's-a-hole-in-your-pants moments. I'd talk to Sean about Valentine's Day, since it happened to be the fourteenth. I knew when I got home I'd find a box of chocolates on my dinner plate, the same Valentine that my Dad gave my two sisters and me every year. I'd tell Sean about that. Maybe he'd think it was sweet. Maybe he'd have a Valentine's Day tradition in his family he'd want to tell me about. Maybe we would converse like real, live human beings again.

In the lunchroom, I scanned the ocean of feeding teenagers for his curly head. Sean wasn't sitting in his usual spot, and a quick walk around the cafeteria revealed he wasn't sitting in an unusual spot either. I tried to hold back the disappointment that welled up inside me. I knew there were three minutes between seventh and eighth period where I'd see him in the hallway on his way to CP Spanish. I could squeeze in my Valentine's Day chat then, if I cut some details.

I sat with a group of freshmen on the ground against the wall of the lunchroom and wished the minutes away as I chewed my soggy turkey sandwich. I knew Sean had recently started hanging out with a group of seniors and realized he had probably snuck out with them to eat over-cooked hot dogs in the parking lot of the 7-Eleven. Seniors were allowed to leave school grounds at lunch; juniors, like Sean, were not. But that rarely stopped him from leaving when he felt bold or bored enough. *What does it feel like to not give a fuck,* I wondered as I picked at the wet bread on my sandwich. Sean was so, so good at it, and I both admired and envied it.

When I finished my lunch, I stood up and wandered over to the hallway to wait for the end-of-lunch bell. I talked to another freshman while leaning against a locker, trying to not feel overwhelmed by the hours of class I'd have to suffer through before getting to see Sean and deliver the speech I had painstakingly rehearsed. Then someone tapped my shoulder. I turned around.

It was Sean. He was holding out a single red rose.

"Happy Valentine's Day," he said.

I opened my mouth to speak but nothing came out. I took the plastic-wrapped flower from him and managed a small, muffled "Thank you."

"You're welcome," he said, and he turned to catch up with his friends down the hallway.

I looked down at the flower, stunned and silent and screaming inside my head. I knew he bought it at 7-Eleven. I didn't care.

The next few hours of class went by in fast-forward.

He liked me. A red rose on Valentine's Day doesn't mean "Let's be friends and have more awkward conversations about my boxers in front of the vending machine." It means all those nights I lay in my bed on the edge of sleep thinking about him, he lay in his thinking about me. It means he felt the same flutter in his chest when he saw me in the hallway. It means he wanted to take me to prom, to dance with me, to kiss me. And not on the chin. He liked me, he liked me, he liked me, and I was crazy about him. So why did I suddenly feel terrified?

When Sean handed me the rose it felt like he handed me the keys to our relationship, like he was saying, "I've taken us as far as I can and now it's up to you to decide where this is going." But I was convinced I would take those keys and Thelma-and-Louise us straight off a cliff. I had somehow tricked Sean into thinking I was a normal, cool girl. But underneath my human clothes, I was thirteen twitchy squirrels darting around and screaming at different frequencies. How could I handle being his girlfriend if I was only just barely handling being a human?

So I avoided him. In person, anyway. I hid behind mountains of schoolwork and three-hour softball practices and babysitting in the time left over. We still spent countless hours talking over AIM, which was my way of staying connected while keeping a safe distance away.

Over many chat conversations, Sean and I grew closer still. Eventually he knew everything there was to know about me—my favorite thing to order at a diner (turkey club on wheat toast), my favorite movie (*Wayne's World 2*), my second-favorite movie (*Wayne's World*), my favorite way to fall asleep (on my stomach, hands under pillow, feet crossed)—everything except what it was like to spend actual time with me. And when our respective sisters kicked us off the computer for hogging it all evening we'd retreat to our bedrooms, eyes still burning from the screen, to call each other from the safety of our sheets. I would listen to his voice dissolve into gravel as the hours passed and we learned more and more things about each other (favorite flavor of Italian ice: Lemon, me. Coconut, him). There was one night we talked so long I shushed him midsentence because I heard the distinct sound of birds chirping outside my bedroom window.

"Do you hear that or am I losing my mind?" I said.

I could hear Sean's steady breath over the phone while he listened. "Oh shit," he said with a tired, disbelieving laugh. "Shit, yeah, I guess that means we should say good night."

"Or good morning," I said, and he laughed again. God, I would've stayed awake for a hundred days to hear that laugh.

We hung up, and, as the morning light began to break, I drifted off to the sounds of the dawn chorus and my own thundering heart.

It went on this way for months, until school ended in June and the free-for-all known as summer vacation began. Without the excuse of school and practice and homework, I very quickly ran out of places to hide from Sean. And then one day he invited me to the park, and I bravely thought, why not? I had survived park hangouts before. How much could go wrong in a public park anyway? I accepted, and then asked who else was going.

I thought we could just go. Alone, he wrote.

My hands clammed up as soon as I read that last word. It was too late to make an excuse. I had already said I'd go. So I did what any socially functioning human being would do: I stood him up.

An hour later I got a text from him. You here??

I agonized, smacking myself in the forehead with my phone before typing back, No.

??????? from him.

`I'm sorry,` I wrote. `I couldn't make it.`

`Why didn't you tell me?` he asked.

It was a good question, one I didn't know the answer to.

`I don't know,` I answered truthfully.

`Kinda fucked up,` he wrote.

My stomach tightened. I knew if I played it wrong, this could be the end of whatever tiny thing he and I had rebuilt. And this time, it would be over for good. I had to make it right. The sky-blue convertible was speeding toward the cliff.

`You can come over. I live near the park,` I wrote. I wanted him to say yes as much as I wanted him to say no.

I waited with my eyes closed, breathing through swells of nausea, for a response.

`What's your address?`

Sean pulled up to my house in his gold Camry less than five minutes later. I greeted him at the back door, the door we use unless we're signing for a package or talking to Jehovah's Witnesses, and led him into the house. We were the only ones home. There was nothing to do at my house, obviously; there's nothing to do anywhere when you're fifteen and seventeen and live in Oradell, New Jersey. I brought him to the living room and I turned on the TV. Disney's *The*

Emperor's New Groove was playing. I told him I used to love the film when I was younger.

"What's it about?" he asked.

"A talking llama," I said. I pictured myself as a tiny infant sitting next to a full-grown man.

We sat in silence on my parents' black leather couch not so much watching the TV as simply existing in front of it. In my head I was planning escape routes, and I didn't dare think about what he might be planning. I so badly wanted him to kiss me, but I was also terrified that he would. It's not like I had never kissed anyone before. I had kissed five other people, thanks to a combination of truth-or-dares, spin-the-bottles, and ex-"boyfriends" (who, between the ages of twelve and fifteen, were just boys I had things in common with and sometimes smushed my face against). But I had never liked anyone as much as I liked Sean. And for some reason, that made kissing him feel like it would be either the start or the end of my entire existence.

Then, without ceremony, it happened. Sean leaned in front of me and tilted my chin toward his and kissed me. His lips weren't matched with mine and his tongue was moving too fast and I felt a bit like a giraffe straining to reach a leaf the way he was holding up my face, but it was still The Best Thing That's Ever Happened to Me. In the background the talking llama screamed, but all I heard was the rush in my ears and the wet sounds of our mouths. I couldn't believe it was happening, even as it was happening. Sean's tongue! In my mouth! Slippery and wet like a slug in the rain. When we broke apart half a minute later we just sort of stared at each other, unblinking. Then he kissed me on the forehead and told me he had to go.

I walked him to his car, though I'm not sure my feet ever touched the ground. We kissed once more against the driver's-side door of the Camry. This time our lips found their marks and their rhythm. He told me he would call me later, and I told him I looked forward to it. I watched him drive away down the street I had grown up on until his car was just a beige blur at the end of the road. Then I turned, ran inside the house, and vomited my lunch into the kitchen sink.

We didn't know it at the time but that day, June 20th, the day I stood him up, made him watch a children's movie, made out with him, and then puked in the sink, would become our anniversary.

We've celebrated eleven June 20ths since then. I wish I could say in those years Sean has revealed that he, too, was nervous and anxious and scared all those months before we got together. That he went home and puked in his own sink after kissing me. And we could laugh about how our neuroses always seem worse on the inside than they look on the outside. But, alas, this is reality. It turns out Sean had approached our courtship with the same calm, relaxed attitude that had drawn me to him in the first place so many years ago.

"Yeah, to be honest it kind of bummed me out that you acted like that," he said when I asked him about it recently. We were taking turns spitting toothpaste foam into the bathroom sink of our shared apartment, a morning ritual that started when we moved in together three years ago. "So I decided I would treat trying to date you like a full-time job until you caved."

Ah, young love.

DON'T READ THE COMMENTS

In the fourth grade I got my first job, and it was total crap. I mean that literally. A woman paid me and my neighbor, Little Erin, ten dollars to pick up the dog poop in her backyard once a week. Not ten dollars each. A single ten-dollar bill that we were expected to split with—what? The extra cash we kept in our wallets? We were eight and ten years old. The money she gave us was all the money we had to our names, not counting the Communion and birthday checks our parents squirreled away for us in mysterious bank accounts that we heard about but never saw.

Despite the pay, we liked having a job, or at least, we liked the *idea* of having a job. It made us feel like we were characters on a Disney Channel show, even if those kids had jobs making Oreo milkshakes at a coffee shop and ours required making direct eye contact with countless mounds of animal excrement. And anyway, we felt like we owed the woman. Before her husband passed away he used to hand out full cans of generic-brand soda every Halloween. Full cans! Do you know what it's like to eat a pillowcase of fun-sized candy and then wash it down with twelve ounces of Cola-Cola or Sprike or Dr Papper? Helping the woman out was the *least* we could do.

On our first day we walked around the woman's backyard on tiptoes trying to avoid stepping on the organic land mines that seemed to cover more of the lawn than the grass itself. I would scrape the poop off the ground with an inside-out plastic bag and then plop it in a paper bag that Little held open with her head turned away. Then after ten turds we'd switch positions. We quickly realized the best pieces of poop to go after were the old ones that had fossilized and turned white from weeks of baking in the sun. They were dry and light and required less scraping, and therefore less hand-to-turd interaction.

We figured that first day would be the worst day, since we were working through a backlog of crap. But somehow each week the poop continued to multiply almost exponentially. It didn't matter how many pieces we picked up; we just couldn't keep up with the rate the dogs were making it.

We tried throwing some in the bushes or mashing the dry pieces into the grass, but nothing worked. There was always more poop. We were twin Sisyphuses rolling white turds up the mountain for eternity.

We soon became resentful of the work. It didn't help that we had used our first couple of paychecks to buy our boss a stuffed dog from the pharmacy near our house as a way to say "thanks for the job." It also didn't help that every week the woman offered us Fudgsicles—a treat I would have said resembled dog turds even before I became an expert on them—and we were too polite to decline. But everything aside, picking up crap is no way to spend a Wednesday evening. And ten years old is too young to hate your job.

I was watching Little wipe a particularly wet pile of light-brown poop off the grass when I decided we had to quit. She was younger than me, and I felt it my duty to make the call for both of us.

"Erin," I said. She looked up from the crap puddle, already frowning. "Let's quit."

"Thank you," she said. I couldn't tell if her eyes were welling up from the last half hour of gagging or from happy-crying.

We bought a pack of gum from the pharmacy with our day's earnings and taped a note to it that said, "Sorry we quit. —The Erins." We left it in the woman's mailbox and never went back again.

After that, I made sure to choose jobs with minimal turd handling, but that didn't mean the jobs were any less crappy. I babysat throughout most of high school, worked at the town pool in the summers, and catered throughout college. I got used to work that involved standing for hours and coming home covered in various liquids. I had a lot of mean bosses who felt no guilt over exploiting young people for cheap labor, and I became all too familiar with two-figure paychecks.

I tried not to complain because I kind of assumed that whatever career I ended up choosing I would suffer for, like my parents did and their parents before them. That's why it's called work, right? Because it's a constant struggle for forty years until retirement or the sweet kiss of death relieves us.

Which is why I'm still surprised I managed to get a job at BuzzFeed, where I wake up every day feeling lucky to go to work and have not *once* been asked to pick a dog turd off the ground. That may seem like an unnecessary thing to say, as most grown-up jobs don't require their employees to pick up dog turds, but over the years we've had a lot of dogs come to the office, famous or otherwise.

The other day I got up to use the bathroom and a man leaning against the wall of the video studio said to me, "Hey, did you see the puppies? There are, like, ten puppies over there," and then did a "heh, heh, heh" laugh. It took me a full second to realize the man was Seth Rogen. "Yep!" I told him. "I was just pretending to go to the bathroom so I could walk by and pet them." That's what some days are like working at BuzzFeed: puppy piles and famous actors around every corner.

My job is weird. I still find it hard to explain what I do to people over the age of thirty. If I had to summarize it, I'd say I compile the best of the Internet into lists for people to read when they're bored at work. I may start out my day by seeing a photo on Tumblr of spaghetti stuffed into someone's wallet, and then three hours later I'll find another picture on Reddit of spaghetti in a copy machine, and then by quitting time I'll have twelve more photos of spaghetti in weird places and make a list of the "14 Times Spaghetti Lived By Its Own Damn Rules." That's a real post I made that three-quarters of a million people have read.

On days I'm feeling ambitious, I'll write lists without any images so that when I tell people at a party, "I'm a writer for BuzzFeed," I can sleep peacefully without the *w* word haunting me like a bad *Sesame Street* graphic. I am given free rein to write about any topic I'd like, which means I have published a list of the "29 Things You Should Never Do When Banging a Dude" on the Internet for all the world to see. This includes (1) Grip their penis like a microphone. Tap the head twice and say into it, "Check. Check. How's everyone feeling tonight?" and (4) Flip them over on their stomach and play their butt like a set of bongos. Wear a black turtleneck and nothing else.

On days I'm feeling less ambitious (read: hungover), I may compile a list that's a little more image heavy to save myself (and the Internet) from trying to put words together. That's what I was doing on the morning of June 18, 2014, when I found myself Googling "Malta" for the first time in my entire life. The thought process had started out easily enough. I was thinking about the oatmeal I had for breakfast, which made me think of old people, which made me think of my late grandparents, which made me think how all four of them never knew me as an adult, which made me think what I would say to them if I ran into them (you know, in a dream or while hallucinating wildly from extreme food poisoning), which made me think of my job, which made me think, wow, I would have to explain the Internet to them, which made me think about their scope of understanding the technological world, which made me think of how much has changed since their childhoods, which made me think of Ireland and Russia and Poland and, finally, of Malta, the homeland of my maternal grandfather.

I had heard the story of my grandfather's immigration to the United States a hundred times. He came over on a boat when he was just a tiny infant, but got sick halfway through the journey. It got so bad that the passengers built him a bread-loaf-sized coffin because they assumed he would die before docking in New York. He survived, though, because the captain nursed him back to health with goat's milk. And after all that, once my grandfather made it safely to Ellis Island, an immigration agent sloppily dotted the wrong letter in his last name, Agius, and our family name became Aguis—a word devoid of country or history.

I knew all of that, but I didn't even know what Malta looked like. So, I Googled it. And, surprise, it's the most gorgeous place my eyes have ever beheld. It's like the love child of Santorini and Rome, but with really cute boats in the harbor. I was in awe that my grandfather's family left that beautiful Mediterranean wonderland to live in Valley Stream, New York. Not that Long Island isn't great. But, seriously. The place looks like a preloaded iPhone background.

It occurred to me it was my duty to let the entire world know of my discovery—or at least the 150 million unique visitors to BuzzFeed dot com the website. I spent the day building a post called "14 Pics That Prove Malta Is the Most Underrated Country in the Mediterranean," because a quick survey around my office revealed most people had never even heard of it, although a shocking number of people had heard of the dog and the falcon and the chocolate treats that look like Whoppers' wealthy European cousin.

I went to bed that night feeling like I'd done my job well enough not to get fired for one more day. And then I woke up to a biblical flood of Facebook notifications.

It seemed my post had found its way back to Malta, and the people of Malta were (wait for it) overjoyed to be featured on BuzzFeed. I went back and reread the post pretending I was a fifty-five-year-old Maltese fisherman whose nephew sent the link to his AOL account. I instantly regretted using phrases like "lucky motherfuckers" and "makes you want to punch yourself in the face." It felt a little like saying something aggressively nice about a kid in class you don't know very well, like, "When Jim reads from the textbook out loud, his voice is like warm choco-late and I want to bathe in it," and then turning around to find Jim standing right there. Sure, it was complimentary, but it still makes you want to set yourself on fire for a few minutes.

I clicked through my Facebook notifications and started responding to the Maltese people who had reached out to me. I even linked up with a long-lost cousin, who said people on the island couldn't stop talking about the post. And then I discovered that someone had started a Go-FundMe account called "Get Erin 2 Malta." *That's so nice*, I thought. *A Maltese person wants me to visit.* Then I clicked the link and saw the campaign had raised several hundred dollars by a handful of donors. Oh shit. A *lot* of Maltese people wanted me to visit.

On Twitter, Maltese people were thanking me for putting their country on the map, which was weird, since I used a map to find their country in the first place. Five-star restaurants and hotels Tweeted to let me know they would host me once I arrived. Then someone Tweeted a photo of the national newspaper of Malta that had a giant photo of my face under the headline: "Campaign to Thank Woman for Extolling the Virtues of Malta." I immediately made it my Facebook profile photo.

As the week wore on, the tides shifted a little. Proud Maltese writers published think pieces wondering who exactly is this Erin Chack and shouldn't we be proud of our country without her? Before long, I began to wonder the exact same thing: Who the fuck *am* I? One writer for

Malta Today wrote an article berating me for playing on the emotions of a small country just for a free trip. I felt like a jerk, until I remembered that I never asked for a trip, and that while he got to write mean articles from a literal island in the literal sun, I've had to stab a cockroach to death with a chef's knife in my apartment in Queens.

Eventually, I made contact with the man who started the GoFundMe. He explained the Maltese people are known for their generosity and hospitality, and they wanted me to experience that firsthand. I didn't have the heart to tell him BuzzFeed's ethics policy restricts us from accepting gifts in exchange for our posts. Instead I let the buzz die down, and eventually the post and the uproar it caused faded back into the fabric of the Internet, never to be heard from again.

It's scary to think about how far of a reach we have at BuzzFeed. The number of people who read my lowest-performing posts would fill Madison Square Garden, twice. So the worst thing I've ever written had a bigger audience than a Taylor Swift concert. But since I never see any of their faces, it's hard for me to believe that that's true. Ask me to read at your wedding, and I will have nervous diarrhea for the three days leading up to it. Ask me to write a post detailing the time I tried to hook up with Sean while listening to "Monster Mash," and I'm like, can we add images, too?

The disconnect between post and real person happens in both directions. Our readers often forget that the people making lists for the site are just that: *people*. This is easy to see when scanning the comment section at the bottom of every post. Readers often refer to the author of a post as just BuzzFeed, as in "I didn't like this post, BuzzFeed. Please try harder." Hi! I'm not BuzzFeed. I'm a twenty-seven-year-old woman who goes to bed at eleven and can't handle more than one cup of tea a day or I'll get the shakes. Telling me to try harder makes me lay my head on my desk and count backward from thirty. Imagine if that happened with any other job? Picture a customer at a restaurant marching back to the kitchen, kicking open the door, and yelling at one chef, "I didn't like this pasta primavera, Olive Garden. Please try harder!" That person would be in jail. Mean People Jail.

It's not isolated to the comments, unfortunately. If a writer includes a picture of a beagle in a list of the "31 Cutest Dogs That Have Ever Lived," someone will write them a strongly worded email informing them (A) It's not a beagle, it's a Hamiltonstövare, and (B) they deserve to have their eyelids surgically removed for confusing the two. I thought by now, after years of receiving countless emails, Tweets, Facebook messages, Instagram DMs, and—yes—even a text saying that I am the dumbest, ugliest, most worthless flesh puddle to ever seep onto the Internet, that I'd have grown a thicker skin. But it still brings a rush of blood to my cheeks to receive a disapproving message, even after all this time. Whenever it happens I try to take a second to wish that person peace in their heart, since they are obviously going through some dark shit if they need to take it out on me, or BuzzFeed, or whomever they think makes the posts. And then I try to do two nice things for strangers that day to balance out the Negativity Debt™ the mean commenter created.

It's also why I appreciate—no—absolutely *love* when people say something nice in the comments. I want to play each and every nice commenter a rendition of "Wind Beneath My Wings" on a golden harp every time they grace the bottom of one of my posts. Thank you, nice commenters, for being a force of good in this sometimes cruel, Hamilton-stövare-owner's world.

I feel awful for complaining because I know as I write this that there's a doctor getting puked on during a double shift. I have a really cool job. I work with really cool people. It's an absolute privilege to write for the Internet, a place almost as weird as the inside of my brain. It's a dream come true to go from being the girl who silenced lunch tables in high school for saying something too goofy to having my bosses say, "This post is so goofy. Let's promote it on all our socials."

People often ask me when I think I'll leave my job. I don't know the answer, nor do I like to think about it, but I guess it will be whenever it stops being fun. There are bad days when no good ideas come to me and I think, *That's it, I'm dried up. Take me behind the Internet shed and end it. I have nothing left to write.* And then a commenter will email me, "Excuse me, you giant idiot, it's Willem Dafoe, not William Dafoe. Do you get paid to write this, you giant idiot? Have I mentioned that you are, in fact, a giant idiot?" And I'll think, I could just work on a farm in the Pacific Northwest herding goats and minding my own business and no one would ever be mad at me for not being funny enough or for messing up the spelling of a celebrity's name.

But then I'll get back to my desk and find an email from a coworker. And it'll be a photo of a cat with its head stuck in a tissue box. And I'll laugh so hard I'll cry. And then I'll make a list of the "39 Cat Pics That Make You Laugh So Hard You Cry." And it'll get a million views from a million real, live people. And I'll go to the canteen to help myself to a bowl of celebratory frozen yogurt. And I'll think to myself, *I love my job.*

RENA OR BEAR?

Five months after graduating from college, I decided to go on a cross-country road trip starting from my hometown in New Jersey to Seattle to Los Angeles to New Orleans and back again. I had decided on the proposed ten-thousand-mile loop around the continental United States after realizing the best way to get my friends and family to stop asking me when I was going to get a job was to drive very far away from them.

But I couldn't do the road trip alone. Ten thousand miles is a lot of miles to drive by yourself, especially when you don't own a car. Thus, I launched my campaign to get my boyfriend, Sean, and our friend Jordan to join me.

Getting Sean to agree to come was easy enough. I held up covers of skate magazines and said things like, "Don't you want to see Venice Beach in person? Aren't you curious what it feels like to stand on top of Burnside?" It was shameless emotional manipulation, an obvious appeal to the softest spot in his heart. He had devoted his life to skateboarding, a culture that started in the dried-up ditches of the West Coast. He had to go, I argued. It was his ordained pilgrimage.

It was much harder to get Jordan on board. When he wasn't convinced by the skating thing, Sean and I resorted to begging. Jordan was the funniest person we knew in real life, and we figured the countless hours spent on the road would go by more quickly if we spent them laughing. Jordan resisted at first, but eventually he must have sensed we really needed him, because one day in late summer he called to tell us he wasn't enrolling in a fall semester at our community college.

"You're coming?!" Sean and I squealed into the phone.

"Yeah, yeah, I'm coming," he said. "But if we die, I'm gonna be so mad."

We set off on our trip with only a few possessions: Sean's ten-year-old Toyota Camry, a tent, a camp stove, some sleeping bags, very little money, and absolutely no plan. On the day we left, my mom stood on the curb twirling her fingers around her ears yelling, "You're LOCO CRAZY," while my dad silently snapped photos of the Camry's license plates with his iPad.

Early on, we had made the decision that we couldn't spend any money on hotels. We needed every dollar to go toward gas (and food, when it was completely necessary), and wasting multiple ones to lie unconscious in a Best Western was just bad financial planning. This left camping and couch surfing as our only lodging options. In the absolute worst-case scenario, we slept in the car, which isn't really sleeping as much as it's taking a series of connected naps in a Marriott parking lot until the sun comes up and hotel guests judge you as they walk by.

We didn't really have an itinerary besides experiencing as much of America as possible and not going back until we hit the Pacific Ocean or ran out of money. We spent the days gunning the Camry toward cities we'd heard about but never visited before, like Pittsburgh and Indianapolis and Milwaukee, and then, once we got there, walking around with nothing to do. Still, we were having a blast. Just talking to people who said "y'all" unironically was enough to keep our spirits elevated.

But somewhere in western Wisconsin I started getting an uneasy feeling, almost like vertigo. It felt as if I had walked out too far on a tightrope and made the mistake of looking down at the ground. In a few miles we'd be crossing the Mississippi River, and I would officially be the farthest west I'd ever been in my life. I had wanted the trip to be wild and unplanned, but I wondered how much chaos I could invite into my life before things got out of hand. Everything we'd done up to that point had come with an escape hatch: We were still close enough to New Jersey to get home in a day, if we had to. But once we crossed that river, things would be different. We'd truly be on our own.

In Madison we tried in vain to catch my sister's friend's burlesque show and ended up sitting in an Arby's for most of the evening recharging our phones. With nothing holding us in the city, we realized our best bet for shelter was camping at a state park fifty miles north.

We arrived after dark and passed countless CAMPERS MUST REGISTER signs on our way into the park, which we chose to ignore. We decided, rather philosophically, that as long as we left the place just as we found it and moved along in the morning, no man could rightfully charge us to sleep in the wilderness. It was our God-given right as human beings—nay, Americans! Plus, it was October, the off-season. And there was no way a person would be collecting money this late at night.

After picking a campsite near the back of the lot, we

got to work setting up the tent. I could sense the boys were feeling as excited as I was to spend our first night camping. Since leaving New Jersey four days earlier, we'd stayed on couches that belonged to friends, friends of friends, and Reid's grandparents, who only served decaf coffee and made Jordan and Sean share a bed while I slept alone several rooms away. Finally, we were going to get the real road trip experience. Fresh air! Bonfire! Peeing on trees!

"Do you think we'll hear any hooty owls?" Jordan asked as he unfurled his sleeping bag.

"I think they're just called owls," I said.

"I've never heard a real hooty owl in my entire life," Jordan said.

Sean dropped a pile of wood next to the fire pit. "Forget the owls, dude. Look at these stars!"

We all looked up. I nearly jumped at the sight of it: a blue velvet sky pinpricked with a thousand twinkling lights.

"This is much nicer than that one star we have at home," I said after a few moments of quiet adoration.

"It's giving me a star-boner," Jordan said.

"A starner," Sean said.

They pointed at each other and smiled. I rolled my eyes.

Once camp was set up, I cooked chili on the single burner while the boys lit the fire. We feasted next to the crackling blaze, and when all the food was gone, switched over to drinking can after can of light beer.

"Isn't it weird"—Jordan paused to take a long sip of his beer, belched, and continued—"isn't it weird that all the roads in America are connected? Like my driveway in New Jersey is connected to a beach parking lot in California. Isn't that weird?"

"That is weird," I said.

"Totally weird," Sean said.

It went on like this for hours until we drank all the beer and the fire reduced itself to embers. We sat in silence, but right as I was about to suggest we go to bed, a soft hooting floated down from a tree above our heads.

Jordan's face lit up.

"Do you hear this shit?" he whispered, pointing his empty beer can at the sky. "Freakin' hooty owls! I knew it!"

"Holy shit, dude. You called it," I whispered back.

"That's it, I'm going to sleep. Nothing will top that. Freakin' hooty owls," he said again.

Sean peed out the smoldering embers while I packed the empty cans and chili pots into a crate.

"Don't worry about that. We'll get it in the morning," Sean said, his speech slurred from too much beer and too little sleep.

"We gotta put the crate in the car so we don't wake up to a raccoon party," I said.

"Oh, in that case, good idea."

The crate stunk of chili, but I decided to put it on the front seat of the Camry anyway. The car had already collected an array of odors on the first leg of the trip; the chili would be an improvement, like a meat-scented air freshener. Once the crate was safely locked up in the car, I crawled into the tent next to Sean to pass out on top of my sleeping bag.

That thing happened where I shut my eyes and opened them less than one second later, only it was actually many seconds later. Hours, in fact. It took me a moment to realize I wasn't at home in New Jersey, and I wasn't looking up at my bedroom ceiling, and the loud, crunching footsteps that had woken me up wasn't the sound of my little sister creeping down the hallway to use the bathroom.

I tried to roll over and find a patch of ground comfortable enough to go back to sleep when a sick feeling crept up my spine. Why was someone walking so close to our tent? It had to be around five in the morning. Were they lost on the way to the bathroom? Or drunk? And if so, couldn't they go be lost and drunk somewhere else?

The rustling persisted. If someone was trying to rob us,

they were out of luck. Our only possessions were a crate of old chili, some skateboards, and duffle bags of clothes that desperately needed laundering. If we got robbed, we would probably be better off.

That's when I heard the low, deep, definitely not human grunt. Oh, holy fucking fuck. It wasn't a drunk thief. It was a *bear*. A real-life bear, lumbering only feet from where we lay. And if I had to guess, he wasn't there to rob us of our shitty stuff. He was there to murder us. Bear style.

I tried to lie very still as the bear sniffed around the campsite, but my body started shaking involuntarily like a cell phone on vibrate. I was literally trembling with fear, which was an expression I'd heard a million times without ever having to confront the truth of what it meant until this very moment.

My mind raced with the facts: This was definitely a black bear, the same kind we have in Jersey. Black bears are skittish, overgrown squirrels that wouldn't lay a paw on a human *unless* the human got too close. That was the problem. We were too close. The bear was definitely looking for food, but I'd packed the crate safely in the car. So was he smelling *us*? I remembered my mom telling me black bears have an excellent sense of smell, even better than dogs. They could smell a strawberry-scented shampoo on the heads of hikers from miles away, she'd said. We were covered in chili-stink and day-old fast food. Did he think we were three overgrown hotdogs in a nylon tent package, and was he about to rip off the wrapper and gobble us up?

We were going to die. We were going to die, and it was all my fault for dragging everyone on this road trip. The irony of surviving cancer just to get slaughtered by a bear would have made me laugh if I wasn't so goddamn scared. In that moment I didn't waste time hoping the bear wouldn't eat us, I only hoped he'd eat me first so I wouldn't have to hear Jordan and Sean screaming as he feasted on their guts.

My shaking intensified, causing Sean to stir next to me. He blinked his eyes open, and I watched as he slowly became aware of me, trembling in the dark. He squinted, struggling to make sense of the situation. I held a finger to my lips, my eyes wide and terrified.

"*What?*" he whispered.

The bear grunted. Sean's eyes doubled in size to match mine.

"*Bear,*" I mouthed.

He nodded. We lay staring at each other, unmoving, and listened as the bear plodded around the campsite for what felt like a lifetime. We were powerless, a couple of greased-up kebabs on a buffet table, and all I could think was *This is really happening*, over and over like a bad mantra.

Just as I was deciding which photo of me I hoped my parents would send to the newspaper, Jordan threw open the flap of his sleeping bag and stood up.

Sean grabbed his arm and pulled him back down to the ground.

"What the fuck are you doing, man?" Jordan asked, gruff and half-asleep.

Sean clapped a hand over Jordan's mouth.

"*There's. A. Bear. Out. Side. The. Tent,*" Sean said as quietly as he could. Jordan looked at me for confirmation. I managed to nod despite my quivering.

"Fuck you guys, I have to pee," Jordan said, standing back up. This time we both yanked him down.

At that very moment, the bear huffed impatiently outside the tent and Jordan's face contorted with fear. "You guys are serious?!" he whisper-screamed and dove between us.

We lay in a petrified huddle, clinging to each other and holding our collective breath for hour-long seconds. I tried to steady my breathing to resist a full-blown panic attack, but after a few more minutes, I started to grow indignant. Just *kill* us already! Pop our heads off like corks and slurp up our insides, but don't make us wait.

If we had just parked the car on the left side of the tent, we might've been able to run for it and dive inside. How silly that we were going to become piles of bear crap in two to three days because we'd parked the car on the right.

Wait. *The car.* Suddenly I had an idea.

"Sean," I whispered. "Are the keys to the Camry in the tent?"

He nodded.

"Give them to me," I said.

Sean reached over to a pocket sewn on the tent wall that held our phones and wallets and handed me the keys. The bear grunted in our direction.

The panic button had never seemed so literal until that moment. I pushed the tiny red square on the back of the clicker and held my breath. Twenty feet away the Camry came alive, honking its horn and flashing its lights. We heard the bear take off in the direction of the woods, the sound of its heavy paws hitting against the ground like drumbeats.

I got up and ran out of the tent, screaming and waving my arms just to make sure the bear got the message, even though it was already long gone. Sean and Jordan joined me in seconds, doing the same. I clicked the panic button again and the Camry fell silent. When we realized we were in the clear, we turned toward each other and group-hugged, relieved to be alive.

"So hyped that's over," Sean said, his voice muffled by the hug.

"Me, too," I said.

"Me, too," said Jordan. "But can you guys stop squeezing so hard? I've never had to pee more in my life."

When we woke up a few hours later, we investigated the campsite. Next to the tent I found an unopened box of granola bars, the cardboard shredded to ribbons, the eight bars completely missing, wrapper and all. The box had probably fallen out of the crate when I was struggling to load it into the car, and the bear had smelled the treats, even through all that packaging.

"That's what he was after?" Sean asked when I showed him the remains of the box. "Jesus Christ, we almost died over chocolate-chip Chewy bars."

I took a walk to the bathroom to brush my teeth and to clear my mind. I had been worried that we were pushing our luck with this road trip, and last night pretty much confirmed it. But was it good luck or bad? Sure, it was bad luck to encounter a bear, but it was good luck that we had survived. It was like when I had cancer and everyone told me how "lucky" I was to have Hodgkin's, a highly treatable form. Lucky! To have cancer! So maybe there was no use in worrying about luck if it just came down to a matter of perspective. If we turned around and went home, our luck would follow us, so we might as well enjoy the rest of the trip. We might as well cross the Mississippi with confidence. We might as well walk out on the tightrope and look straight down.

I returned to camp to find that a state trooper had issued us a formal warning for sleeping in a state park without registering first. Luck, you son of a bitch.

The only music we had besides the radio were three songs Jordan had downloaded to his phone: Billy Joel's "Vienna," Bob Seger's "We've Got Tonight," and Bad Company's "Bad Company"—the daddiest of all dad rock, but our only reprieve during the long stretches of static. We listened to them on repeat as the landscape faded from fall foliage to dusty plains to rocky mountains. We saw wild bison and Mount Rushmore and snowcapped peaks. We stayed with our friends' parents in their beautiful lake houses and our friends' friends in their shabby college apartments. We got a shopping bag full of free bagels from a cafe in Sioux Falls.

We got a speeding ticket in Coeur d'Alene. We got closer and closer to the Pacific Ocean with each passing day.

Three weeks into the trip, we hit Washington, our very first West Coast state. We yelped and high-fived and felt like the pioneers, except probably better since no one in our caravan had died of a rattlesnake bite or cholera. Then somewhere outside Spokane I got a text from an unknown number.

> 360: hi! u dont know me, but i got ur number from Brandon in montana and he said ur making ur way through the Seattle area and will need a place to stay. u can stay with me if u want! i live alone in the woods on the olympic peninsula and ur welcome to my floor/stove/bathroom.

Brandon was a friend of a friend of a friend we had crashed with in Missoula, Montana. He was a vegan transition skater who allowed us to spend two nights on the secondhand couches on his screened-in porch. But he hadn't mentioned hooking us up with a place to stay in Washington. This text had come completely out of nowhere.

I turned down Bad Company and read the text aloud to the boys.

"That's . . . nice . . ." Sean said.

"Yeah, a little *too* nice," Jordan said.

"Should I text back?" I asked.

The entire trip we had been scrambling to find a place to sleep every night. Sometimes we'd be driving around after midnight, wearily looking for any patch of grass to pitch the tent. Other times we would spend the entire day calling people we barely knew. "Hi, remember me? Do your parents still live in Wyoming? No? Well, are your grandparents still alive?" But now that we had a free place to stay, we were unsure if we wanted it. It was like having no food in the house, opening the door to go to the grocery store, and finding a perfect cake sitting on the doorstep. We weren't above eating a stoop cake, but we'd have to do a little investigating before digging in.

Instead of texting the number back, I texted Brandon. He explained that the person who had texted me was a girl named Rena, and he had met her when she crashed on his couch a few days before we had passed through. When she heard we'd be traveling her way, she immediately asked for our numbers so she could offer to let us stay, too.

"It's just, like, *waaay* too good to be true," Jordan said. "Like, does she realize there's three of us? And we smell terrible? And we have no money to give her in exchange for this?"

"I can tell her if you'd like," I said, holding up my phone.

"Yeah, it's not like she's a friend doing us a favor. She knows Brandon, who is friends with Naomi, who is friends with Luca, who is friends with us," said Sean.

"'*I live alone in the woods,*'" Jordan continued. "What do you think she means by that?"

"That she lives alone," I said. "Probably in the woods."

"Or," said Jordan, "that she's the mastermind behind a series of torture games, like in *Saw*. You've gotta read in between the lines here. 'I live alone,' if you don't count the bodies I've buried behind the garage, 'in the woods,' where no one will hear you scream when I torture-kill you."

"Have we considered that maybe she's just really nice?" I sighed.

"Nice people are a myth," Sean said. "Just like Helen Keller."

I rolled my eyes. "Not the Helen Keller thing again."

"You don't believe in Helen Keller?" asked Jordan.

"Please don't get him started," I interjected. I caught the boys exchanging a look that seemed to say, *We'll talk about this later.*

"We don't have anywhere else to stay," Sean said.

"I'm down if you're down," I said.

Jordan sat back with his arms folded. "Fuck it," he said. "Let's do it. Let's get triple murdered."

I texted Rena back.

We arrived on the peninsula after dark. Rena's cabin didn't have an address, which meant we couldn't use our GPS to get there. Instead she asked us to meet her next to a chain-link fence near a lake in the woods, which was exactly one mile from a generic-brand gas station. We couldn't miss it, she explained. It was the only chain-link fence around. She told us she would be waiting at the fence in her car and would lead us back to her cabin from there.

"I do have to admit, this is getting a little more murdery," I said as I pulled the Camry off the country road onto the shoulder near a rusted old fence.

A second later, a pair of headlights flashed twenty feet up the shoulder.

"Uh," I said. "Should I flash back?"

"Yeah, flash her!" Sean yelled.

Instead I rolled down the window and yelled, "Rena?"

I heard a hearty laugh ring out in the darkness. "Yeah, hey! Sorry, I don't know why I did the headlight thing. OK, follow me!"

We followed her little blue VW a little farther down

the road before turning down a path between two trees and taking a nearly vertical dirt road up to her house.

Once our Camry crested the hill, I could see the cabin, cozy and glowing, nestled between the trunks of two giant trees.

"Um, this is adorable?" I said as I parked next to Rena's hatchback.

Jordan squinted. "Yeah, a little *too* adorable."

"OK, Jordan, you have to draw the line somewhere. You're suspicious of everything."

"Yeah, a little *too* suspicious," he said, darting his eyes back and forth.

I giggled and killed the engine, kicking the car door open to meet Rena.

If Rena was a murderer, she didn't dress like one. She was wearing cutoff jeans and an oversized flannel jacket covered in band patches. She had bracelets up to the middle of her forearm and a streak of blond in her thick brown hair. She looked like an anti-murderer, like she went around stabbing the life back *into* things.

We shook hands. Rena, the gang. The gang, Rena.

"Thanks for coming out, you guys," Rena said as she walked us toward the cabin. "I know it's a little hairy getting here. This is really the country out here."

"No, no, we should be thanking you," I said. "I don't know where we would have stayed tonight."

"Yeah, well, Brandon said you guys were having trouble finding places to sleep. I couldn't rest knowing you weren't making only good memories of Washington. No bad vibes, you know?"

We agreed, although it still seemed *really* nice of her. If someone came to New Jersey and had a less than perfect time, I would hardly consider it my fault.

Inside the cabin we tossed our backpacks on the ground and took it all in. Rena's place was set up like a studio apartment—bed and stove in the same main room, bathroom off to the side—and tidily kept. The shelves were full of stacks of mixtapes with handwritten song lists and homemade zines with women skaters on the covers. A coffee table shellacked with bottle caps sat tucked against the wall. Flannel and jean jackets hung neatly from a hook on the closet door.

"Make yourselves comfy," she said. And we did.

We sat around the kitchen table drinking beers and eating spaghetti out of water glasses because Rena had no clean bowls. I tucked into my cup, grateful that she had accepted our pasta offering without going through the polite protests of "Oh, no, I couldn't, well, OK, if you insist," or apologizing for not having the right receptacles.

At one point Rena cracked open a fresh beer and got up to go to the bathroom, leaving it fizzing on the table between the three of us. I thought about all the times I'd been warned not to leave my drink unattended around strangers and how it was clear Rena had never learned any of the stranger rules like (1) Don't talk to them and (2) Don't invite them to sleep in your home. Earlier that day I wondered if Rena was going to murder us, and now I was the one thinking how easy it would be to mess with her drink. Her trust was disorienting.

We talked until midnight, the three of us in a semicircle around Rena, who sat cross-legged on her chair and slapped her knee whenever she liked something we said. We told her about the bear and the worst places we'd slept. She told us about her own bad road trip experiences and started stories with phrases like "Back when I was an anarchist in high school . . ." She drew a map on the back of an envelope with all the places where we could skate the next day and where to get the best egg sandwich. She gave us homemade stickers and a copy of her favorite zine. Then, a quarter after midnight, she stood up from the table and announced she was leaving.

"Leaving? Wait, where are we going to sleep?" I asked, realizing, *Ha! It* was *too good to be true!* She had baited us here just to kick us out when it was too late to find another place to stay. We'd have to drive back to Seattle and spend another night shallow-napping in a hotel parking lot.

"You're sleeping here. I'm a caretaker for a woman in town and my shift starts early, so it's easier for me to sleep over at her house," Rena explained.

"You're leaving us here? Alone?" Jordan asked.

"Don't worry, I'll leave the bathroom light on for you guys."

"But we'll see you in the morning?" Sean asked.

"Actually, no. Not unless you're still here at three P.M."

"So this is it?" I asked.

"This is it," she said.

That night, we lay in our sleeping bags on the floor of Rena's Rena-less cabin all stuck inside our own heads. It was weird to think we might never see her again, despite begging her on her way out the door to visit us in New Jersey, an offer she politely laughed off. If I had known we would only have such a short time with her I might've done something drastic, like take her photo or ask for her autograph, anything to make our brief connection more tangible. More real.

"I miss Rena," Jordan said, his voice slicing through the dark silence. We agreed.

The next day we drove until we hit the Pacific Ocean. We stood on a rocky beach with our hands clamped on each other's shoulders, unable to believe we had done it, we'd crossed a continent, from sea to shining sea. The ocean looked a lot like ours at home, but the morning sun stayed to our backs, like we had somehow flipped the sky upside down. *How incredible the world is*, I thought, *how incredible the people are who live in it.*

After that, we began to think of our luck as either Bear or Rena.

In Portland, Oregon, we stayed with Sean's friend's stepmother, who pointed a manicured finger to the back-yard and said, "You can set up your tent next to the chicken coop. Watch out for the dog shit though." I awoke that morning to the silhouette of her Labrador's curved back, a single turd dangling from his butt, projected on the wall of the tent just inches from my head. That was Bear.

In Pismo Beach, California, we let the air out of the Camry's tires to camp next to the ocean and stumbled upon a community of people who drive trucks on the dunes for fun. We got a free ride up and over a wall of sand in an ex-marine's pickup. That was Rena.

A parking ticket in New Mexico, Bear. A two-for-one sale on six-packs in Louisiana, Rena.

After five weeks our tour came to a close and we rolled into Jordan's driveway, the same one that connected to the beach parking lot in California, and said goodbye. Home was home. I still didn't have a job, and I wouldn't find one for months. In fact, the only thing that changed was my age, after I celebrated my twenty-third birthday in a gas station outside New Orleans. But the night we returned from our ten-thousand-mile trip it started raining, and the next day it rained even harder. Our parents told us how lucky we were to get back when we did, because the news was saying this storm was serious. A superstorm, in fact. They gave her a name, Sandy, and I thought of the dunes in Pismo Beach.

Our town lost power for nine days. Water flooded basements. Trees smashed through roofs. The governor postponed Halloween. We spent the days waking up with the sun, walking around in circles, and going to bed when it grew dark. There was nothing to do and nowhere to do it. Our world had shrunk from a continent to a small, wet cave.

Getting home in time for a hurricane. Was that Bear or Rena?

IT'LL GROW BACK

I got the second-worst haircut of my entire life in a Florida shopping mall when I was eight years old. We were there visiting my grandparents, who had moved into a retirement community like all people from Long Island are legally required to do once they hit seventy. It was called Sun City Center, both the town and the community, which to my eight-year-old mind sounded like a metropolis straight out of a cartoon. I imagined yellow rays of sunlight glinting off a skyline of enormous, glassy skyscrapers. In reality, Sun City Center looked more like one giant golf course interrupted by the occasional two-story condo. Still, it had palm trees. That was cartoon-y enough for me.

My parents had billed the visit as a vacation to my sisters and me, but really we had gone down so my mom could help my grandparents settle into their new living situation and quietly grapple with the fact that they were officially Elderly and probably going to die in the sun-bleached wasteland known as western Florida. Because my parents had a lot to take care of, enjoying the "vacation" was 100 percent a personal responsibility. My older sister, Elizabeth, took this to mean holing herself up in the air-conditioning while listening to Goo Goo Dolls CDs on her Discman and rereading *Chicken Soup for the Teenage Soul* for the third time. My little sister, Emily, still a fat-legged toddler at this point, spent the week strapped to my dad's back in the Babybjörn running errands with our parents. That left me to lie alone in the crab grass outside our grandparents' condo, baiting tiny lizards with fruit snacks or begging Liz to chaperone me at the over-chlorinated community pool.

Halfway through the week, when my mom had a break in her erranding, she decided we would all go out for a seafood dinner near the beach—our first real vacation activity. I attempted to look presentable on my own, but when it came to my hair, I couldn't drag a brush through it. Three days of chlorine and sun had left it tangled beyond reckoning. I knocked on the door of the guest room where my mom was getting ready, the brush dangling from the back of my head like the tail of a coonskin cap.

My mom tried to hack through the chlorinated haystack attached to my head. Forty minutes later, we were running late to our dinner reservation.

"Didn't you use cream rinse?" she asked, yanking on a particularly stubborn snarl near the back of my neck. I told her I hadn't shampooed or conditioned my hair since we left New Jersey. We were, after all, on vacation. She pulled a tiny leaf out of my hair and held it up to me.

"That's it," she said. "Tomorrow you're getting a haircut."

The tone of her voice should have been a warning, but I was overjoyed. A haircut! What a perfect accessory to go with my brand-new tan.

The next day, my regularly scheduled grass-laying was interrupted by a trip to the mall with my mom. During the car ride there I told her I already knew what haircut I wanted. Layers. Like Liz had.

"Oh, you'll get layers alright," she said. I smiled and settled back into my seat.

What I actually got was a pageboy, hideous and short. Technically there were layers, they just happened to start above my ears. I stood in the middle of the mall crying openly, performatively, knowing I was embarrassing my mom but also knowing she'd never feel a fraction as embarrassed as

I felt with that god-awful haircut. My pain was her pain, I decided. She had brought this upon both of us.

My mom tried to calm me down, reminding me that hair grows back and in the meantime I wouldn't have to worry about it tangling or accidentally collecting samples of various flora and fauna. Short hair meant freedom! Short hair meant happiness!

The spectacle attracted the attention of a middle-aged Floridian woman who happened to be passing through the meltdown zone. I had accidentally made eye contact with her while taking a breath to gear up for a particularly earth-shattering wail.

"What's wrong?" she asked, walking over. Various shopping bags dangled from her tanned forearms.

"Tell her," my mom said, her patience just a memory at this point.

"I . . . hate . . . my . . . hair . . . cut!" I yelled between my emotional hyperventilation.

"Aw, sweetie," she said, leaning forward to rest a warm palm on my shoulder. "You are a very handsome little boy."

For eleven years after that I never cut my hair shorter than my shoulders. At my most adventurous I experimented with bangs, but they were long and side swept and could be easily blended into the rest of my hair on days I felt they were "too much." The only thing more unremarkable than the cut of my hair was the color, which was firmly committed to being neither fully blond nor fully brown. I looked aggressively ordinary. If someone had taped a brondish medium-length wig to my locker, my friends at school would have said, "Hey, Erin!" as they walked by.

Then, when I was nineteen years old, between flashbacks of a certain mall in Florida, I chopped my hair to my chin. Like the time in Florida, it wasn't by choice. An oncologist suggested I cut it to lessen its weight on my scalp and lower the chances of my hair falling out from the chemotherapy treatments for my Hodgkin's lymphoma. Afterward I took the dismembered ponytail, still tied at one end with a turquoise elastic, and stuffed it into a padded envelope to send to a charity that makes wigs. Their website promised I'd get a postcard confirming they'd received the donation, but I never did. I often imagined a man sitting at his breakfast table, opening the day's mail, tearing open a mysterious package, and screaming bloody murder.

When I started my chemotherapy treatments, I had steeled myself against the possibility of losing my hair, but after going through the first two treatments without shedding a single strand, I started getting cocky that I would be among the lucky few that kept their hair. My oncologist had said I *may* lose it, not that I would. Of course, he was using conditionals to minimize accountability—typical doctor-speak. Still, I latched onto the "may" like a baby fist on a finger. I figured keeping my hair would be the silver lining to the worst thing that would probably ever happen to me.

It wasn't. I was sitting in my friend Reid's gray Wrangler outside my house when I realized my hair might be, maybe, definitely falling out. We had just come back from eating bagels in a parking lot and were finishing up our conversation before I went inside to take my daily nap (cancer has *some* perks).

"But you're feeling good?" Reid asked.

"Yeah, I feel alright. I get treatment once every two weeks, so I only feel *really* shitty for three or so days of the cycle," I told him as I absentmindedly ran my hand through my hair. I noticed with each stroke a few hairs would get caught between my fingers. I shook the strands out through the open window. Was that normal? It wasn't uncommon to lose a strand or two when I was playing with my hair, but with every stroke? I couldn't remember.

A breeze blew through the car window, warm and scented like the hyacinth in my mother's garden. It was late June, but today was the first nice day after what felt like a solid month of rain. People were outraged at the weather—June is usually the best month in New Jersey, and they felt cheated. I didn't mind though. The outside matched my insides.

"What's wrong?" Reid asked. I realized I had stopped listening and was looking down at four strands of brown-blond hair in my open palm.

"Look," I said, offering my palm to Reid. "My hair, I think it's coming out."

"I don't know, my sister's hair is always everywhere. I think that's a girl thing."

"Yeah, but *look*," I said, tossing the hairs out the window and running a hand through hair at the back of my head. Three more strands stuck between my fingers. I showed Reid.

"See?"

Reid scrunched up his face.

"It's probably fine," he said. "There are, like, hundreds of thousands of hairs on your head. I don't think losing a couple hairs every time you touch it will matter."

But the next day a couple hairs became ten, then fifty, then hundreds. Showering was the most devastating; the pressure of the stream would pull full locks out of my head until a wet, rat-sized clod of my hair stopped up the drain and the gray water rose to my ankles. While I slept, my hair would stick to my pillow like it was covered in flypaper, and I'd wake up with the strands caught in my eyes and throat. Every day I wrapped my hand around what was left of my ponytail to check its thickness, only to find with each passing day I could clench my fist tighter and tighter until there wasn't enough hair left to grip.

My hair didn't fall out evenly, as I expected it would; I had imagined it becoming thinner and thinner until nothing was left at all—a gradual disappearance, the way snow melts. But instead it fell out in random patches and chunks, which somehow made the already unnerving process more unnerving. One day I got out of the shower and glanced in the mirror to find that my hairline had jumped back a considerable inch. The skin at the top of my forehead where the hair had been was pale, creating a faint border against my tanned face like a cranial bikini line. I tipped my head forward and back, side to side, checking from every angle. Yep, my normal hairline was gone. Just *gone*. I looked like a nineteen-year-old Mr. Belding.

In my bedroom I pulled on the same pair of sweatpants I had on before the shower, pausing between each motion to look in the mirror and frown at myself, hoping that my teenage-pattern baldness was a mirage or a trick of the bathroom light. But no matter how many times I checked I still had a whole inch of forehead that wasn't there before the shower.

I had just put on a dirty T-shirt when I heard the bottom stair creak. I knew immediately from the weight and distribution of the sound that it was Sean. I'd lived in that bedroom for nearly twenty years and had developed a sixth sense for knowing who was coming up the stairs.

Thirteen more creaks followed the first until Sean was standing in my room. I turned to him.

"Hey-ahhhh," he said as he made eye contact with my new hairline. "You look . . ." But he couldn't finish because I had walked over, stuffed my face in his neck, and started whimpering.

"No, no, no, no," he said, shushing me and rubbing my back. My shoulders shook and I dissolved into sobs. It was the first time I had cried since before my diagnosis.

"Hey," Sean said, pulling back and resting a hand on each of my shoulders. I let my head hang limply, the patches of remaining hair obscuring my face. He ducked down to look into my eyes.

"I love you, OK?"

I stopped crying. Not because of the power of love or

anything, but because a new emotion had bloomed in place of the self-pity. Anger. At myself. In the last month I had been assaulted with countless needles. I had been pumped full of caustic, stomach-turning chemicals. I had spent a week in a hospital bed after my white blood cell count dropped to zero and missed Sean's twenty-first birthday. I had a nurse take a pint of blood from my femoral artery because all my other veins had collapsed. I had bone marrow sucked from my pelvis while I lay conscious on the table. I had to mentally prepare myself that, despite all this treatment, all the pain and all the agony, I might still die. And *this* was what I was crying about? My *hair*?

I wiped my nose with the back of my hand and looked at Sean. "Let's go for a drive," I said.

We cruised around aimlessly through the spiderweb of streets that made up our suburban town. Sean scanned the radio with one hand and steered with the other. I rested my head on the window ledge and gazed at my unfamiliar reflection in the side-view mirror.

"I look like Frankenstein," I said.

"Hey, that's not true," Sean said. "You look like Frankenstein's *monster*."

He covered his mouth to hide his laughter, but his eyes

said, *Sorry, had to.* I pulled a chunk of hair from the back of my head and placed it gingerly on his thigh. He looked down in horror.

"Ew, dude!" Sean said, scrambling to throw the hair out his open window like it was made of spiders. The car swerved, and I laughed.

"Aw, don't do that," I said. "Someone's gonna find it and clone me, and then you'll probably dump me when we're forty to date her."

"Oh, what an investment. Give me more?" he said, putting his palm out.

I turned away.

"I gotta get rid of it," I said. I rotated my head from side to side to assess the damage in the mirror. Patches of dark-blond hair fell to my chin. My scalp was visible in random spots, and my hairline seemed to creep back farther before my very eyes.

"Alright, let's make an appointment," Sean said.

"No, I don't think I can handle walking into a salon like this."

"You probably just need to buzz it anyway."

"Yeah, I think Nicole across the street has clippers," I said. "Her boys always have buzz cuts."

"Text her," Sean said.

"Eh, I'll text my mom," I said. "She can ask for me. Save me the embarrassment."

We were in luck; not only did my neighbor have clippers, but her mother was a hairstylist and in town for the weekend. I felt strangely comforted that the person who would be shaving my head was a professional, even though in my heart I knew that Nicole's youngest son could operate a buzzer with his left hand just as well.

The next morning, I sat in a plastic lawn chair on the patio behind my garage while my mom draped a threadbare pink towel over my shoulders.

"Should we put something on the ground to catch the hair?" I asked.

"No, we can let it go," she said. "The birds will use it to make their nests."

My dad came out of the house holding a thick orange extension cord, which he plugged into the outlet on the back of the garage and left the other end coiled at my feet. My parents pulled up matching plastic chairs and sat facing me.

"HEY, IS TODAY THE DAY?" a familiar voice called from the adjacent yard. Little Erin's mom, Kate, was walking over to us. Her husband, Mike, was trailing behind.

"WAIT FOR US," a voice yelled from a window in the house on the opposite yard. Soon a small army of my neighbors was congregating on the patio, pulling plastic lawn chairs off a stack in the corner and forming a semicircle around me. I looked at everyone facing me. There was eighty-year-old Jose Luis and his wife, Rose, and their daughter, Maria (whose thick, black half–Puerto Rican, half–Italian hair seemed to taunt me); Kate, Mike, and Little Erin; and my two sisters and my parents. *Dang*, I thought. *We should have charged admission.*

As if on cue, Nicole and her mother appeared from around the garage. Her mother was holding an unmarked black plastic box by its handle. It looked like a miniature prop suitcase from an action film.

"I'm Karen," Nicole's mom said as she transferred the box to her other hand to shake mine. "I wasn't expecting an audience."

"Neither was I," I said.

"Well, too bad! Ya got one!" Kate yelled. The neighbors cheered.

Karen placed the plastic box on the patio table and unclipped the latches on the handle. She lifted the lid to reveal the red enamel hair clippers nestled in foam, the cord folded neatly beside.

"Have you, uh, ever shaved a head before?" I asked.

"Yes, I have," Karen said, pausing as she turned to plug the clippers into the extension cord. I could hear the ellipsis hang in the air. ". . . But you're the first girl."

With a click the clippers hummed to life.

"I thought we'd start with a number two and go shorter from there if we need to," Karen said.

"OK," I said, wondering what a number two was.

Without preamble or permission, she brought the clippers to my temple. There was murmuring among the neighbors. I felt the first lock of hair slide down my cheek and brush my neck before floating to the ground. I was glad she didn't wait to start. I don't know what I would've said or thought or felt. Another lock fell past my ear.

There was no mirror, so I watched my neighbors' faces to monitor how things were going. Their smiles got tighter and tighter with each stroke of the clippers, like someone was turning a crank attached to the corners of their mouths. I couldn't handle the silence.

"How's it looking?" I asked just to fill the air, knowing I wouldn't get an honest answer.

A moment passed before anyone spoke.

"Good!" Maria chirped, nodding her head too quickly. Her hair bounced around her shoulders.

Karen stepped back from my chair and looked at me. She cocked her head to one side and squinted.

"You know what? I think we should just use a zero," she said, not waiting for me to agree. She popped a plastic attachment off the head of the clippers and resumed buzzing. I could feel the cool metal on my scalp.

It didn't take long. After all, I didn't have much hair to start with. When Karen finished, she stood back, blew a cloud of tiny hairs off the clippers, and said, "All done."

I pulled the towel off me and let the patches of my hair float to the ground where they gathered into clumps. I watched as the breeze rolled them a few inches down the patio. I traced their path with my eyes; at the other end of the patio, dark-blond tumbleweeds were tangled in my mother's garden, clinging to the tulips and daffodils.

"Looks cool!" Kate said, breaking my trance.

"Very cool," my sisters said in unison.

"You did so good, E-Mo," my mom said, using a childhood nickname I rarely heard anymore. She squeezed me against her.

I stepped back and brushed stray hairs off my shoulders and hers. "Thanks, guys," I said. "Hope you enjoyed the show."

Karen had already packed up the clippers when I

walked over to her. "Thank you for doing that," I said. "It makes life much easier."

"Please," she said. "Don't worry about it." She snapped down the latch on the plastic box and smiled with her mouth closed. I never saw her again after that day.

As my neighbors started to file out of the patio, I reached up to feel my hair. My hand could feel the cool skin of my scalp, and my scalp could feel the warmth of my palm. I realized I had never felt that sensation before in my life.

My dad walked over to collect the extension cord. He patted me on the back.

"You OK?" he asked.

"Yeah, I'm good," I said. "Hey, didja ever think I'd have hair shorter than you?"

I don't know why I thought he'd laugh, but it felt so weird when he didn't.

"No," he said. He bent down to pick up the end of the cord and started wrapping it around his forearm.

I turned and walked back to the house as casually as I could, not wanting anyone to think I was anxious to see how I looked. When I got inside, I squeezed my eyes closed and turned to face the mirror that hung next to the door. I knew when I opened them things would be different. Even though my head was already shaved, it didn't count as reality until I saw it. I wondered if I'd forget what I once looked like, if this new version of me would replace the old one, like saving over a computer file.

I opened my eyes. I saw my face, the one I had known for nineteen years, and around it was . . . nothing. Empty space. The absence of hair. It was like someone had stretched my forehead over the top of my head and erased all the familiar boundaries. I thought I'd still have hair—very, very short hair, but *hair*. What I had was mostly skin, the same as the inside of my wrist, with patches of fuzz in random spots around my head. It looked like a map of a world I didn't know with great, wide oceans of scalp. I ran my hand over my head, over the patches, and little golden hairs shot out like sparks. My hair was still falling out. Even at a sixteenth of an inch long it couldn't stay put. Which made me realize: I would somehow be balder than I already was. It would get worse.

Right then I heard the high-pitched squeal of a bad engine belt outside the door. The Camry. Sean was here. He knew I'd be shaving my head that day, but in my desperation to get it over with I had forgotten to tell him exactly when. I heard the driver's-side door slam and I panicked. I didn't want to shock him, didn't want his first reaction to my shaved head to be one of confusion and disorientation.

I ran into the kitchen to look for something to cover my head and spotted a tea cozy, still hugging the teapot in the center of the breakfast table. It was cream colored, except for the dark splotches of old tea stains, and covered in illustrations of cats napping. I yanked it off the pot and tugged it onto my head; the insides still held the warmth of the morning's tea. It felt oddly good on my scalp, which was still getting used to the constant chill without my hair.

I ran outside to meet Sean, who had made it just feet from the back door.

"Hi," I said.

"Nice hat," he said.

"I, uh, well. It's gone," I said, pointing up at my head. "My hair."

"I figured," he said, stepping toward me. He pinched the top of the tea cozy between two fingers, shut his eyes, and pulled. He, too, wanted to remember the file image before it saved.

He opened one eye, then the other, then his shoulders fell down to their normal height and he smiled.

"Oh," he said. "You look beautiful." He pulled me toward him by my wrists and kissed me.

"I look bald," I said when we broke apart.

"Yeah, but still beautiful," he said. He reached up to touch my head. "I love these little patches. You look like a cheetah."

"Don't get used to them," I said, demonstrating the spark trick.

He shrugged. "Either way."

The next morning, Sean didn't come over at the normal time. I only noticed because I had started looking forward to hearing his car squealing outside between 10:30 and 11:30 A.M. every day. It was summer, and without school or jobs to fill our time, our only plans were to walk around on the days I felt good and drive around on the days I felt bad. But that day he was late, and I wondered if maybe everything was beginning to weigh on him. The baldness made the whole ordeal real in a way we hadn't yet experienced. It's not that I thought he'd break up with me—he kind of couldn't, or he'd be the guy who dumped the girl with cancer—but I'd understand if he needed a day away from me, a day to skate with his friends and pretend things were normal.

I texted him, Where you at?

Sorry, had some stuff to do this morning, be right over, he texted back.

I lay in the hammock in my side yard noting the way the breeze tickled the places where my hair had been and waiting to hear the Camry pull up. And then, finally, it did. The engine cut, the car door slammed, and his footsteps approached the hammock from the concrete walkway.

"You're late," I said as I sat up to turn and face him.

"Sorry," he said as he came into my view. "I was getting my hair cut."

His face seemed off, a little too big, and then I realized it was because it didn't have the usual crop of long, curly black hair hanging around it. His scalp gleamed in the sunlight.

"You . . . shaved your head?" I asked dumbly.

"Yeah," he said. "You like it?"

"You shaved your head," I repeated, standing up.

"Yeah," he said, laughing.

"You shaved your head, you crazy idiot!" I said, tackling him.

"Yeah!" he said, falling over, though he probably didn't need to. "So did you!"

"We look like lunatics!" I said, sitting on top of him and aiming punches at his stomach as he batted my fists away.

"I know!"

I stopped punching him. "Thank you."

He hugged me around my middle. "Of course."

I stayed bald for the better part of a year. Eventually my eyebrows and eyelashes fell out (and for those inquiring minds, yes, pubes, too), and I moved from the realm of Maybe She Has a Really Daring Sense of Style to Definite Sick Person.

Finally, I had my last chemotherapy session in November. In December I was granted remission status. In January I re-enrolled in classes at my university two hundred miles away from home. By then my hair had started to come back, fuzzy and baby-like. I had three short, stubby eyelashes on each eye and the faint outline of eyebrows. After seven months of being balder than a basketball, this felt like a huge improvement. I was practically a woolly mammoth.

But being back at school forced me to see myself from other people's perspectives. And the other people were appearance-obsessed twenty-year-olds at a private university. Suddenly the hair on my head felt even less substantial than a crew cut, not so much a hairstyle as a thin covering, like a scab over a wound. One time I tried to fill in my eyebrows with an eyeliner pencil that I didn't realize was shimmery, and I sat through an entire class with twin glittery comets etched across my forehead. Another time a girl I had known from freshman year asked me in the dining hall, "Why'd you cut your hair?! I liked it long."

"Me, too," I said, excusing myself to cry quietly in the quesadilla line.

After about a month of exchanges like this, I was exhausted. I missed Sean. I missed my family. I missed the bubble of comfort I had at home. So one weekend in late February, I took a bus home to New Jersey. It was around my mom's birthday, and I figured I could hide my loneliness behind the purpose of celebrating with her. I needed to live inside the soft walls of the bubble again, where no one's eyes drifted up toward my hairline, even if just for a few days.

But as soon as I got home, my dad called me into the kitchen. I sat down on a creaky wooden chair while my dad stood in front of me with his arms crossed. I was confused because he seemed agitated, or angry, until I realized it was a third emotion I still don't have a name for.

"We have to tell you something important," he said, even though he and I were the only ones in the room.

"OK," I said.

"Mom found a lump."

"OK," I said again.

"She has a biopsy in two days."

"OK."

I felt scared, and then angry, but then I did the math in my head: The odds of me getting cancer were slim; the odds of us both getting cancer were slimmer. The odds of us both getting cancer in the same year were nearly impossible. She couldn't have cancer. It made no sense. There was simply no way it was true. This lump was most likely a fluke, a funny story we'd tell people years from now when I had hair down to my shoulders, an urban legend from our family history.

In March I had my first checkup since going into remission. My mom started chemotherapy that same day.

I wasn't there when my mom lost her hair; I found out via text message while I was alone in my dorm one afternoon. I don't know who shaved her head, I don't know if she sat outside on the patio behind the garage, I don't know if the neighbors were there or if they cheered. What I do know is the Greek word for "homecoming" is *nostos*, because that's what I was doing when it happened—studying Ancient Greek and other useless, inapplicable bits of knowledge I have never needed to know.

When I got the text I went outside and sat in the tiny rectangle of grass in front of my building on Buswell Street in a fading patch of late-day sunlight. I called my mom.

"How are you?" I asked.

"Oh, just very bald," she said. She sounded tired but still like herself.

"I know," I said. "I'm sorry."

I paused and gritted my teeth before saying the next thing.

"Mom, I'm gonna shave my head. I promised myself if anyone close to me ever got sick I'd do it. I just . . . didn't expect to have to do it so fast."

"Erin Maureen, don't you dare," she said. "You just got that hair back. Don't go shaving it off."

It wasn't a polite dismissal; it was a mother's order. And I was relieved, honestly, to be given the out. My hair was starting to get to a length where it looked like a real, pre-meditated hairstyle. The baby fuzz had been overtaken by actual human hair, and it was full enough to push to the center and spike into a little faux-hawk with the help of men's pomade. A girl in my Media Law & Ethics class com-plimented me on it. She said she wished she could pull off hair like mine. It was the first time I had felt pretty in almost a year.

But my relief was quickly swallowed up by shame. My mother had taken me to every appointment, kept notes on what the doctor said in a notebook in her backpack, waited for hours during the infusions. She slept on an armchair next to my hospital bed when I stayed for overnights. She drove me places. She paid for stuff. And what had I done for her now that our situation was reversed? Left her to deal with it alone while I went back to school, to normal life.

The only connection I had to her illness was knowing in gruesome detail exactly how it felt. I knew how the Zofran made the room spin and how the bleomycin burned when forced into the vein. We had the same oncologist. We sat in the same infusion chair. I had shared all the things she felt but there was nothing I could do to save her from feeling them. I was useless to her. And it terrified me.

"What can I do then?" I asked. I had to inch forward on the grass to stay in the shifting sunlight. The sunny patch was almost gone, overtaken by shadow.

"Just do your best in school," she said. "That's all we want." I rolled my eyes. What a typical thing for a mother to say.

I got straight As that semester.

A SEA OF KATES

I met my best friend, Alijah, while waiting for an elevator in a London apartment building, but it's not as serendipitous as it sounds. We were both studying abroad for the semester, and like all modern-day relationships, I knew who she was as soon as I saw her because I had already stalked her on the Internet. I had seen her Facebook profile months earlier while my friend Kate and I were selecting our roommates for the program back in Boston. We were sitting in the Student Union picking at a cardboard container of cold crinkle fries when she slid her laptop over to me.

"Should I pick this girl as my roommate?" Kate asked.

On the screen was a picture of a girl dressed as a lion, her blond hair teased and standing on end, her face painted completely orange except for a black triangle on her nose. Her mouth was fixed in a silent roar.

"Yeah," I said. "She seems fun."

I had already picked my roommates: a girl from my home state of New Jersey, because I knew we'd have stuff to talk about, and a girl from Chicago, because I knew we'd have stuff other than New Jersey to talk about. Still, I felt a twinge in my chest when Kate clicked "Accept" on the lion girl's name on the housing website. I was already imagining them painting each other's faces between swigs of English cider straight from the bottle while my Jersey roommate and I talked about which mall we lived closest to.

Six months later I was standing in the lobby of my new dorm building in West London, my bags still packed, my body still on American time, when I saw lion girl waiting by the elevator. It wasn't difficult to recognize her without the costume; she had the same mane of wild blond hair. Maybe it was the jetlag or the loneliness of having said goodbye to all of my friends and family at Newark airport not thirty hours earlier, but I decided to introduce myself.

"Hey," I said. "You're Kate's roommate, right?"

She spun around and regarded me as if I were trying to buy her a drink in a club. I immediately wished I'd said nothing.

"Uh, all my roommates are named Kate, so you'll have to be more specific," she said, not particularly warmly.

"Kate Eberle," I said.

"Brown hair?" she asked.

"Yes," I said. "Jesus, how many Kates do you live with?"

"Three," she said. "It's three Kates and one Alijah."

The elevator dinged and she stepped inside.

"I'm Erin," I said, "no Kates." We shook hands, but she looked generally bored by the formality.

"Well, see you around probably," she said as the doors closed between us. After a second of standing alone in the lobby, I realized I was so flustered I had forgotten to get on the elevator. I ran up the stairs instead.

Class started the next day. I arrived to British & Irish Poetry embarrassingly early and took a seat in the back of the classroom, which wasn't really a classroom at all but a beautiful Kensington apartment that the program had retrofitted with desks and a projector. I checked the gold-faced clock above the double doors, and in the time that remained before class, I ripped a sheet of paper out of my notebook to write a letter to my boyfriend, Sean, at his college in New York.

I had covered an entire side of notebook paper with my sloppy handwriting when I looked up to see Alijah taking a seat next to a boy in the front of the class. From their familiar greetings, I figured they already knew each other back in Boston, two best friends who decided to level up their best friendship with a four-month romp in a foreign country. Alijah seemed so different around him, not aloof like she'd been at the elevators. I watched her unmistakably pantomime changing her own diaper, her legs in an awkward squat as she pretended to remove what appeared to be a very heavy load. The boy played along, puffing invisible baby powder on her butt. I went back to writing my letter, somehow feeling more alone as the classroom filled up.

Studying abroad in London had been my big plan. After recovering from cancer I decided not to pass up any new experiences that came my way, even if they made me feel sweaty and weird. It sounds cliché—the cancer survivor with a new zest for life, next on *Oprah*!—but it's actually just vain. I realized if I had died, my obituary would have been about two lines long: "Here lies Erin. She never even went to Europe. But she did go to Niagara Falls once, which is . . . cool, I guess."

London seemed like my best option. I was studying journalism, so I had to go somewhere I could speak and write the language, which left only England, Australia, and

Canada (and you can't go to Niagara Falls twice. Your eyes will gloss over and you'll walk into traffic and get hit by a car and die).

An English-speaking country also meant I wasn't limited to only hanging out with people in my program. This was important because I'd need all the friendship opportunities I could get. For the first time in my adult life I'd be really, truly away from my friends and family. Not a car ride away, but *away* away. If I didn't jive with the other kids in the program, I had an entire country of people I could befriend. Our common language meant I could theoretically walk up to anyone on the street and say, "Cool face, want to get a beer?"

The decision to go to London was easy enough, but the actual act of leaving ate me up. I had only recovered from cancer a year and a month earlier, and my mom was sixth months into her own remission. I started eyeing the other members of my family warily, wondering which one of them would catch the cancer next. My fourteen-year-old geriatric cat, Ashes, seemed the most susceptible, and I found myself following him around the house trying to assess if he seemed more lethargic than usual.

"Do cats normally sleep this much?" I asked my dad. I was kneeling next to Ashes's favorite sleeping chair watching his furry gray belly rise and fall.

"Erin," he said to me over the top of his newspaper, "there's a reason they call them cat naps."

It sucked the most to leave Sean. We had been dating for six years at that point, and while going to separate colleges in separate states acquainted us with having our own space, putting an ocean between us felt like a little too much of it. And four months was a long time. Leading up to the program, I started having dreams that my plane to England shook itself apart midflight as if it had been held together with duct tape, wings and engines and bags of peanuts plummeting into the ocean from 32,000 feet in the air.

Despite that steaming batch of fresh anxiety, I knew I had no choice but to go. It felt like going to the gynecologist: kind of uncomfortable but ultimately important. I had to go and see Big Ben with my own two eyes. I had to make new friends even though I had good ones back home. I had to . . . because I'd already bought the plane ticket.

And now I was 3,459 miles from home sitting in the back of a strange classroom listening to my poetry professor drone on about the cuff in Prufrock's pants while Alijah and the boy doodled pictures of themselves as babies on the same sheet of paper and tried to suppress their giggling. Two things were readily apparent: First, English poetry is just as exciting as American poetry, which is to say, not very exciting at all. And second, flying halfway across the world to make new friends doesn't guarantee that you will.

The next day I was thrilled to see Alijah in another of my classes, British Journalism: Culture & Society, sans doodle boy. *Perfect!* I thought. Without him she'd be more susceptible to my friendship advances. I tried not to think about her stiff reaction to me outside the elevators and waved.

"Ah, we're two for two," Alijah said, taking a seat in the desk ahead of me. So she had noticed me in Poetry but she had chosen not to say hi. This wasn't looking good.

"What's your third class?"

"Uh, British Film & TV," she said.

"Damn, I'm The Contemporary British Novel," I said.

"I just switched out of that. I heard you have to read a book a week."

"I'm screwed then," I said. "I can't read."

She laughed despite herself just as our professor, an older British man with a slight stoop, shuffled in. He took a piece of chalk into his big red hands with gold rings squeezed on the fingers and wrote his name on the board: Professor MacLeod.

I tapped Alijah on the shoulder.

"MacLeod-y with a chance of sausage fingers," I whispered, wiggling my fingers a few inches above the table.

She snorted.

After class I set off to walk the single block back to our dorms when Alijah called out to me.

"Hey, you know about this shortcut?" she asked. She had stopped walking so I could catch up, the late afternoon sun making her hair glow golden.

"Shortcut?" I asked. "It's a two-minute walk."

"Yeah, I guess it's technically a longcut," she said. "But it's worth it if you've got the time."

I followed her through a gap in the white-columned row houses, down an alley, and onto a cobblestone pathway. Brightly painted garage doors flanked us on either side—the reds and blues and yellows a welcome relief from the pervasive London gray. Outside each door sat huge porcelain planters promising blooms come spring.

"Wow, how did I miss this?" I said. "I've been walking down the street like a chump this whole time."

"Yeah, pretty magical, right? It's called a 'mews,' I think. Ah, yeah, there's a sign—Colbeck Mews."

"Colbeck *mew mew mew*." I was making high-pitched

cat noises before I even realized what I was doing. Heat flooded my face. I felt like I had been just barely reeling Alijah in with ninety-nine-cent dental floss and this display of utter insanity was more than enough to snap the line. Meowing like a cat isn't pretending-to-change-your-own-diaper-with-your-best-friend weird. It was *weird* weird.

"*Mew mew mew,*" she called back.

Back in the lobby of our apartment building, I had already resigned myself to taking the stairs, a charade I felt I needed to keep up for the remaining four months of the program so that Alijah would never realize I had forgotten to get on the elevator the first time we met. As I turned toward the stairwell, Alijah asked if I had plans and, if not, would I like to come have tea on her floor. I wondered if she could hear me screaming "YES!" inside my own head.

"You know, 'cause England," she said by way of explanation, making a sweeping gesture toward the entrance of the lobby as if the queen was pressing her ear against the door.

"Yeah, I'd love to!" I said, probably too enthusiastically.

"Great! David and I have tea this time every day. He only drinks PG tips because Julie Andrews drinks it."

I had no idea what PG tips was, but I knew David

was doodle boy because she pronounced it Dah-VEED. Our Poetry professor, for whatever reason, couldn't seem to get a handle on the pronunciation and called him DAH-vid throughout the entire class. Not DAY-vid—DAH-vid. It wasn't a name so much as the sound a spring doorstop makes when you flick it. I felt awful for him every time.

"Oooh, right. David from Poetry," I said, making sure to get it right. "You two were friends before the program?"

"No," Alijah said. "I met him in the kitchen on my floor. He goes to school in San Francisco. He's one of the few non-Boston kids here. I just think he's awesome because five minutes after I met him he told me he has an alter ego named Sinjin who's like a butler but maybe also a sex freak? It's not clear. His catchphrase is 'But *I* have a question for *you*!' But then he never actually asks one."

This was great news. David hadn't known Alijah much longer than I had, which meant I had time to catch up. And it seemed as though Alijah was actually drawn to the same eccentricities I'd been desperately trying to tone down since high school. Oh, you like weirdos, Alijah? Just wait till you see how I eat a kiwi.

"I'll meet you on your floor," I said, turning to run up the stairs. "I'll bring cookies—I mean, uh, *biscuits*." I cocked an eyebrow and nodded my head toward the door.

✳ ✳ ✳

After our initial teatime, Alijah and I were inseparable: We sat at the same table in class, had tea in the afternoons, walked aimlessly around the city in the evenings, and got drunk in dimly lit pubs at night. In our time together I quickly learned Alijah put a distance between herself and people she didn't know very well because she was protecting an intensely special personality, and only those brave enough to bridge the void were allowed to see it. She was, quite simply, the single most interesting person I had ever met, the kind of girl who would find a scarf on the ground, throw it around her neck, and yell, "The streets provide!" Alijah told me she once picked up a used ChapStick off the street in Boston, sliced off the tip with a strand of her own hair, and pocketed it.

"There are no germs on the unused part," she explained. I couldn't argue with that.

Alijah had names for different sides of her personality, like Lil' Lijy Purplemouth, who came out when she drank too much red wine. She ironically unironically wore maternity clothes as daywear ("They're more comfortable!"). At night she slept with the head of her childhood stuffed bunny because the body had long since disintegrated from twenty years of love.

The more we hung out, the more I realized that around her I could be my full self, the person I was around Sean and my family. Her quirks left room for me to exist without fear of judgment, like there was nothing I could do to make her recoil so there was no use stressing about how to act. And that's true friendship, isn't it? Giving each other space to be your true, weird selves.

The more we got to know each other, the more our relationship seemed destined. We both had younger sisters named Emily. Our dads had the same birthdays, September 8th. And our strongest link: Her birthday was the day I learned my cancer was in remission, December 17th. We decided to call that day Life Day and made a vow to celebrate being decidedly not dead with a good old-fashioned keg party when we were both back in Boston. She was my fated friend, my kindred spirit. She was an alien princess loosely disguised in human clothes. She was an Alijah in a sea of Kates.

It took Alijah and me weeks to become friends, but it took just one night for us to become best friends.

It happened on a Friday in early February about a month after we met. I was laying on the floor of Alijah's dorm while she sat perched on her top bunk, fiddling around on her laptop. We had just returned home from a largely uneventful field trip touring the newsroom at the *Telegraph* for our British Journalism class. The most exciting thing that happened that day was when our professor snapped a photo of Alijah and started chuckling.

"What?" she asked. "What's so funny?"

"I'm sorry, it's just—" Professor MacLeod turned his digital camera around in his big hands so we could see the picture on the display screen. "Alijah, you look so very pleased to be here."

In the photo she is grinning from ear to ear, her eyes electric and wide, her face flushed and glowing. It was the face one might make on a roller coaster, not on a walking tour of an old British newspaper.

"I just love field trips!" Alijah yelped.

"Indeed," he said, laughing. "You look quite like the cat that got the cream."

Alijah and I looked at each other and dissolved into giggles. It was an expression neither of us had ever heard before, but we somehow knew it fit her perfectly.

I was lying on Alijah's floor thinking about that, about how crazy it was to be living in London, to have a professor who spoke in charming animal maxims, to have found a friend who got me, when I heard Alijah growl above me on the bunk.

"What's wrong?" I asked.

"This dude Todd!" she said. From where I was lying, I could only see her feet hanging off the edge of the bed, the bottoms of her socks dirty and gray. "He's a friend of my friend in Boston. He's, like, backpacking through Europe and of course he's in London and of course he needs a place to crash and of course I'm the only one he knows here."

"How long does he want to stay for?" I asked.

"Just a night," she said. "Which is fine! But now he's asking if I'll hang out with him tonight. Show him around."

I recognized this side of her, the one I had met in front of the elevators. She didn't know Todd, so she didn't like Todd. It was her only flaw: reverting to her cold exterior around people she didn't trust. I, on the other hand, have always been great at meeting new people. Years of dulling down my personality in high school made me great at small talk and able to mold myself to appeal to all kinds of people.

I watched Alijah's feet kick impatiently back and forth above my head before clearing my throat.

"I'll go with you if you want," I said.

Her legs disappeared and I heard scurrying from up above. A second later her head popped over the edge, appearing in the spot where her feet had just been.

"Would you really do that?" she asked.

"Yeah, it's no big deal. I was hoping we'd hang tonight anyway."

"Yeah, but this could be so lame. He could be so lame," she said.

"Or," I said, "it could be fun. I'll bring my friend Charlie. We'll just do what we normally do on a Friday night but Todd will be there."

"Are you *sure*?" she asked. She was acting like I'd just volunteered to swap appendixes with her when all I'd done was offer to drink some beers in close proximity to a stranger.

"Alijah, yes!" I laughed. "I'm sure he's great."

Todd wasn't great. He wasn't *bad* either, just kind of dull— the kind of kid who talked too loud and told boring stories. The kind of kid that made Alijah put her walls back up. I stood in her room and watched Todd dump the contents of his giant, dirty backpack onto her floor while the Kates looked on and pretended not to be annoyed.

"Have you guys been traveling at all?" he asked, rifling through the objects on the floor until he found a can of deodorant.

I knew this was a trick, that he had no interest in whether I said yes or no, that he just wanted to talk about his own experiences. I took the bait anyway.

"Yes," I said. "Alijah and I have both been to Paris."

"Ah, no, no, no," Todd said, pulling his T-shirt away from his body so he could fire off a stream of deodorant straight at his pits. "Ya can't go to Paris. It's too touristy! Ya gotta go to Bordeaux. That's where the real French live."

"I can't go to Paris?" I asked.

"Ya, ya just can't," he said, snapping the lid back on the can.

"But I already did go to Paris," I said.

"Ya, but ya can't. Ya gotta go to Bordeaux."

I looked over Todd's shoulder and saw Alijah roll her eyes so hard I thought they'd detach from her optic nerves.

"Erin, is Charlie ready? Please tell me Charlie's ready," Alijah said.

"He's meeting us there!" I said, clapping my hands together a little too loudly. "So let's head out."

"I just need to find my passport," Todd said. He dropped to his knees to sort through the dusty pile of backpack guts.

Fifteen minutes later, with Todd's passport safely tucked in his back pocket (where it had been the entire time), the three of us set out for the tube station at the end of our road. We made a pit stop at a Tesco Express to buy some cheap hard cider because even after a month of living in London, legally drinking cans of alcoholic beverages on the street in plain sight was still our most exciting and exotic privilege.

"Should we just split this four-pack?" I asked, squinting at the foreign measurements on the label. How many twelve-ounce beers were in five hundred milliliters? Why hadn't I learned this yet?

"Better get two four-packs," Alijah said, dragging the clanking cans off the shelf and making her way to checkout without waiting for me to agree.

We each finished a can before we tapped our Oyster cards at the tube. We crushed another round sitting on the train. Then Alijah and I split the seventh while Todd drained the eighth on the walk to the pub.

Charlie was waiting for us inside. He had picked the pub, a place called Filthy McNasty's in North London. He said he liked it because they had live Irish folk music, but I knew he liked it because it was called Filthy McNasty's. Charlie was a friend of Sean's who happened to be studying abroad in London the same time I was there. I met him for the first time in London—Sean had put us in touch—but his connection to Sean made me feel closer to home, so I hung out with him every chance I could. Plus, I wanted him to meet Alijah. And hopefully drown out Todd.

Alijah and I fought our way up to the bar, leaving Charlie and Todd to get acquainted.

"What are you drinking?" I yelled over the chaos around us.

"A lot!" she yelled back. "Sorry Todd's so boring."

"He's fine!" I shouted. "I'm just happy to be hanging with you."

"Me, too!" she said, grinning.

We each ordered a shot and a beer and elbowed our way back to the boys.

After half an hour of screaming at each other over the roar of the pub, Charlie yelled in my ear, "Maybe we should just get some street beers and hang outside!"

I nodded and passed the message on to Alijah.

"Yeah, let's ditch this place!" she yelled back.

Todd just stood there, waiting to be told what to do.

We fought our way to the doors until the crowd spit us out like four watermelon seeds onto the sidewalk. It was only then that I realized how drunk I was, the absence of bar noise like cotton in my ears, the streetlights smeared in my vision. I threw my arm around Alijah. She smiled wildly and leaned her head into my neck.

"I'm wasted," I stage-whispered to her.

"Me, too," she said. Her walls, while still up, had weakened a little under the weight of all the alcohol.

The boys were walking only a few paces ahead of us, but they seemed worlds away.

"Alijah, wait," I said. I had stopped walking.

"Wh-what is it?" she asked.

"Get on my back," I said. I hunkered down, the earth tilting beneath me, so she could hop on. She didn't even hesitate.

I ran, all hunched over and listing, to catch up with the boys. Alijah was giggling in my ear, her arms tight around my neck, her hair tickling my cheeks.

"Hey, Charlie," I said. "This mole on my back wants to know where you're taking us."

"Yeah! Where are you taking us?" Alijah squealed, doing her best impression of a birthmark.

"There's a great kebab place ten minutes up the road," Charlie said. "We can grab beers on the way."

"I'm beered out," I said, trying to keep my speech from slurring. "I just need a bathroom." I had to pee back at Filthy's, but the idea of swimming through the tightly packed bar to find the bathrooms had overwhelmed me. With Alijah's weight on my lower back, I realized the situation was more urgent than I had thought.

"There's no bathroom at the kebab place," Charlie said. "You'll have to find one on the way."

I would have felt dread if I could have felt anything through the bubble of alcohol that numbed my body. The area we were in was largely residential, and it was already midnight. Where did he expect me to find a bathroom?

Alijah hopped off my back, and I stumbled, getting used to how light I felt without her.

"Lij, I gotta find a bathroom. I can't hold it," I said. I took her by the hand and ran ahead of the boys. I dragged her into a pizza place, but the guy behind the counter shooed me out, pointing to a CUSTOMERS ONLY sign. We tried a cell phone repair shop next. I tried to look as sober as possible, begging the workers to let me pee while their faces blurred together in my field of vision, but they just shook their conjoined heads.

Back outside, Todd and Charlie stood with their arms folded, their patience wearing thin. I started to feel embarrassed for making them wait, for not peeing at the bar, for getting too drunk. I also began to resent Todd for instigating the entire evening. Where might I be if Todd hadn't dropped in? Somewhere with bathrooms probably. Fucking Todd.

I looked at Alijah. Everything swirled around her like a watercolor painting, but her face remained steady, constant.

"I'll find you a place to pee," she said. "You guys stay *right here*. We'll be back in a little."

I followed Alijah down a side street, through an alley, and into a parking area between two apartment complexes. It was almost like she knew where she was going, like she had peed there before or was guided by some natural instinct. She pointed to a section of wall in the corner of the lot that was out of the direct glow of the streetlights.

"There," she said. "Pee."

I looked around. The buildings surrounding the lot had windows. Anyone could look out from their apartment and see me.

"It feels kinda exposed," I said. The sound of drunk voices echoed down the alley from the street.

"Pee-ers can't be choosers," Alijah said with a shrug.

I scanned the parking lot. Most of the windows had their blinds drawn. The others were dark. Alijah was right; this was my best option.

"OK," I said. "Keep an eye out."

I planted my feet and pushed my back against the hard brick wall like the wall-sits we used to do in gym class and shimmied my jeans and underwear to my knees. The cool night air breezed past my naked butt and I realized I was way, way out of my element. I had peed outside before but only in nature during hiking or camping trips. This was my first urban pee, and it was an entirely different experience, like peeing on level expert. I looked at the windows opposite from me and prayed they stayed dark. I still hadn't started peeing.

Please pee, please pee, please pee, I chanted to myself. I had held my bladder so long it was difficult to relax enough to let the pee out. The longer I didn't pee, the more nervous I became. *Come on, just pee!* I screamed in my head. My legs started to shake from the wall-sit, my thighs burned.

A few more excruciating pee-less seconds passed, and then like sweet music I heard the unmistakable sound of urine hitting the ground. I looked between my legs. I wasn't peeing. I looked to my left in the direction of the sound. Alijah was wall-sitting next to me, her leggings yanked down to her knees, a forceful torrent of piss exploding from between her legs.

"Wait," I said, barely comprehending. "You had to pee, too?"

"Nah," Alijah said. "I just thought it would be less scary for you if I did it, too."

I laughed so hard that the urine poured out of me. The relief was sweet and instant, like the first breath of air after spending too long underwater. I didn't care anymore if someone caught us. I was so happy. Not just to be finally peeing, but to be peeing with her, in a strange parking lot, three thousand miles away from home.

When we finished I realized I didn't have anything to wipe with, since there were very few leaves in urban peeing.

"How do we wipe?" I asked.

"Oh, I just do a little shake," she said, demonstrating.

I imitated.

"Sometimes I do it at home, even when there's toilet paper," Alijah explained as she pulled up her pants. "Better for the environment."

We skipped out of the alley arm in arm to find the boys where we'd left them on the street.

". . . ya don't understand, it's the wine capital of France," Todd was saying to Charlie, whose eyes had glazed over through no fault of the alcohol in his system.

"Hi!" I interrupted. "Sorry about that. We're ready now."

"Great!" Charlie said, a little too loudly. "Let's get some kebabs."

At the kebab shop we sat around a red square table and dove into our meals. Kebabs, Charlie explained, were the British equivalent of pizza in terms of drunk food: cheap, filling, and available late. I hadn't recognized anything on the menu, so when Charlie had placed his order I added, "Make it two, please!"

"Ya, three," said Todd.

"Whatever's vegetarian!" said Alijah.

We were silent as we dug into our doner kebabs, too drunk and voracious to make conversation. It felt like a victory meal to me, a prize for successfully executing my first urban pee. Also a prize for not peeing my pants in front of three people. My lips tingled with every bite.

"Wait, this is pretty spicy," Alijah said, breaking the silence. Her eyes darted between the three of us helplessly. "Wait, this is *really* spicy."

She pinched a wad of napkins out of the metal holder and wiped her lips. Then she started wiping her tongue. "It's too spicy!" Alijah yelped. I could see the drunken urgency in her eyes; it was the same panic I felt earlier when I realized I had nowhere to pee.

She hopped up from the table and ran to the glass-front fridge full of beverages next to the counter. She scanned the rows once, then twice, and spun around. Her eyes were watering and her face had taken on the scarlet color of our tabletop.

"I need milk!" she cried.

"Grab a water," I said, pointing to the bottles in the bottom row.

"No, no, spice isn't water soluble, it'll just make it worse," she said. Alijah stuck out her tongue and fanned it with her hand. "I need milk. MAMA NEEDS MILK."

She turned to the counter and slammed her palm down. The guy working the register looked at her wide-eyed like he was about to take orders from a wild animal.

"Milk," Alijah said. "I need to buy some milk."

"We don't sell milk," he said.

"Listen, I know you have milk back there. This is a kitchen, right? Please. I just need a cup of milk! Gimme that MILK!"

He hesitated.

"PLEASE!" she cried.

The man backed away from the counter then disappeared behind the curtain that separated the kitchen. Thirty seconds later he returned with a little plastic cup full of milk.

"How much?" Alijah asked, digging into her coat pocket.

"Just take it," the man said, his hands raised in surrender.

"THANK YOU," she said.

Alijah whipped around, cup in hand, and beelined for our table. Right when she made it over to us her foot caught on the leg of her chair and she tripped forward, throwing out her hands to brace her fall.

Time slowed down. I watched in horror as the cup caught the edge of the table and tipped from a vertical to a horizontal position. A white tidal wave of ice-cold milk broke over the table. And finally, the empty cup came to a clatter in the middle of the mess. I could almost hear opera music playing in the distance.

When time returned to its normal speed, I saw Todd and Charlie jump up from the table to avoid the milk river that was flowing in their direction. I closed my eyes, threw my head back, and laughed before I could stop myself. Then I heard Todd and Charlie yelling, "No, no, no, stop! Don't do it!"

Alijah was bent over the table, lapping up the milk with broad strokes of her tongue.

"Just ask for another cup!" I yelled, laughing harder, grabbing napkins from the holder to help contain the mess.

"No time!" she said between licks. I glanced over Alijah's hunched back at a young couple I hadn't really noticed sitting in the corner of the restaurant. They looked like they had just witnessed a murder.

Alijah slurped what was left of the milk puddle while I rubbed her back.

"Aw, girl," I whispered. "I hope you're OK."

Alijah paused mid-lick and looked up at me, her eyes huge and brown, her chin dripping with milk.

"The cat has really got the cream this time!" she squealed.

We got kicked out of the kebab place. Standing on the sidewalk outside, Todd and Charlie patted themselves down with the napkins they managed to grab before we left. I put my arm around Alijah and gave her shoulder a squeeze.

"You are my favorite little kitten," I said, swaying.

She planted a wet, milky kiss on my neck and tucked her head into my shoulder. *"Mew mew mew,"* she said back.

FIND YOUR CARROT

Because I've been in a relationship for over ten years, people often ask me for dating advice. This is dumb, in my opinion. Listen to it when I say it like this: In the past ten years, I've only been in one relationship. Would you ask a guy who's jumped out of a plane one time in the past ten years for skydiving advice? Or would you ask a guy who has jumped out of a plane many, many times in the past ten years for skydiving advice? Think about your options here, people.

I have no idea how or why Sean and I have been dating as long as we have. Every day I wake up and look at his unconscious face illuminated by the clear morning light and wonder: *How the fuck is this guy still my boyfriend?* Not in the "enough already!" sense. More like in the "wow, nice, we're still going" sense. I feel like for the past ten-plus years

I've been walking around with a very fragile dried flower in my pocket, and sometimes I just can't believe I haven't crushed it to dust yet.

People often suggest that the reason we're still together is that we're soul mates, and all I can do is smile and nod. I don't believe that we are soul mates. I don't believe that any two people are soul mates. As if there is one person for every person on earth, and I just so happened to go to high school with mine. What are the odds of that? One in seven billion? I'd have a better chance of buying a winning lotto ticket, getting attacked by a shark on my walk home, and then arriving at the hospital to find out that Kim Kardashian is my doctor. And then we start talking and she's like, "Wait, I think your aunt is my accountant."

If soul mates are real, I think they're not found, as our culture suggests, but made. There's not one person for everyone; there's a ton of people for everyone, and you pick the one you like the best (or the one who lives the closest to your childhood home, like I did—it makes deciding where to spend Christmas way easier). Then you work at being with each other over many years, and eventually, your selves become tangled together. I once saw a picture on the Internet of two carrots that grew twisted around each other, like an orange-y double helix. If I had peeled apart those carrots and showed someone just one, that person would instantly know that the carrot was one of a pair, that it had spent a lot of time hanging out with another carrot, that it was a more interesting carrot because of it. That's what soul mates are: carrots that spent too much time with each other.

Sean and I are good at dating each other. We've worked to become good at it. We are particularly good at communication, which is something I imagine couples therapists stress is important. (I don't know for sure, I've never been to couples therapy. But sometimes I wish I could go just to hear a therapist say, "What are you two doing here? You're great at this!" I am, after all, a millennial, and I thrive on constant validation.) Our favorite activity is getting into a car, driving for hours, talking about our feelings, and helping the other person talk about theirs more effectively. For example, I used to think that the best way to express my anger was by being defensive and saying the most hurtful thing to the other person. I assumed that fights were won by the person who could be the meanest (aka me). Sean has informed me that this is not actually true and that the way to resolve an argument isn't by delivering devastating burns—it's by making sure both people feel heard. It scares me to think how long it would have taken me to figure that out if we weren't together. But dating someone allows you to practice being a better person. It's like juggling or surfing or any other pastime—after doing it for ten years, you start to get the hang of it.

As Sean and I've grown up together, we've dated different versions of each other. At one point in high school, I dated Sean the Disillusionist. This was when he decided fashion was a social construct and wore only white T-shirts, blue jeans, and black sneakers for four straight months. It was like going out with a character from *Hey Arnold!* I loved it. I found his rejection of labels in a school overrun with Abercrombie & Fitch T-shirts to be thoughtful and vaguely James Dean.

One winter in college I dated Sean the Dart Player. After flipping past an obscure ESPN channel and catching a darts tournament one evening, he decided, hey, maybe *I'm* also really good at darts. He bought his own set from a store in town (yes, we're from a town with an entire store dedicated to darts), joined a team, and competed in some truly forgettable Jersey bars. I cared for this less: Practicing for tournaments meant throwing darts with him in his freezing garage for hours, and I have little tolerance for holding metal objects in subzero temperatures.

After college I dated Sean the World's Most Casual Pothead. This lasted for two months, tops. And to this day we argue about the amount of commitment he had to this persona. I remember him lighting up a joint four, maaaybe five times and doing activities like: reorganizing his book shelf, cleaning the space under his bed, sitting on the roof outside his bedroom window and gazing up at the New York City light pollution we call a night sky. He insists he was high for an entire summer. Don't do drugs, kids. They really impair your ability to remember that you weren't high for an entire summer.

I imagine when people date for a month or two, they remember their exes by these temporary identities. "Remember that guy I dated? Sean? The dart player?" When you date someone for as long as I've dated Sean, you see their entire evolution, and you know the darts thing was just one bright thread in the tapestry that makes them who they are. If there's one thing Sean and I've done well, it's allowing each other the space to pick whatever color thread appeals to us at that point in time, even if we're silently thinking, *Ugh, CHARTREUSE?*

Starting a job at BuzzFeed was a pretty bright thread for me. Suddenly I had found my identity as a writer and had all these built-in friendships since BuzzFeed employs a lot of cool and interesting people in my exact age group. Sean gave me space to make these connections, and, during my first year at BuzzFeed, I canceled countless dates to go to more brunches and karaoke nights than I care to remember. I know now I hate brunch and karaoke—getting drunk at one P.M. and eating fifteen-dollar eggs is a waste of a Saturday, and karaoke only exists so that people who can sing can rake in compliments—but I am fond of that time period and the fact that my brunch partners went on to become editors-in-chief, writers for late-night shows, and literal People's Choice Award winners.

But there was this Friday, about a year ago, when BuzzFeed hosted a whiskey tasting in honor of St. Patrick's Day. Most Friday nights I'd stay in the city for a beer or two after work and then make my way home to Queens to grab dinner with Sean. I told him before leaving for work that day not to expect me; the tasting would surely eat up my evening.

My coworkers and I tasted *a lot* of whiskey, and when the event was over, a couple of us tasted even more from the cups that had been filled but not claimed by anyone. It was one of those magical nights where everything clicked: the right mix of people, the right amount of alcohol, the right Friday vibes. At one point my coworker Matt was telling a story and my other coworker Isaac interrupted him mid-sentence.

"Dude, you've got an eyelash," he said, pointing at his own cheek for reference.

Matt brushed at his cheek, but the stray eyelash stayed put.

"Let me get it," Isaac said. He leaned across the table, reached over, and ever so gingerly pinched the eyelash between his thumb and pointer. "Make a wish."

Matt closed his eyes and blew the eyelash off Isaac's thumb. We all watched it float through the air in dizzying spirals until it slipped beneath the table and out of our lives forever.

A moment passed, and no one dared to move. Finally, my coworker Sarah whispered, "That was *so beautiful*," sending everyone into a fit of laughter and reaching for another drink.

We ended up staying at work well after the six o'clock quitting bell. Each hour that passed another coworker got up, cited plans they regretted making, and left, until finally, around nine or ten, I found myself alone in the empty office.

It's weird to be at work when no one else is. All the areas of buzzing activity—the canteen, the bathrooms—are dark and quiet but familiar, like a toy that's been switched off. I took a minute to take it in, the absence of everything. Then I pulled on my coat and walked toward the exit.

Out of habit, I took the stairs. Once I pushed the door to the stairwell open, I felt a cool wind coming from above. I glanced up and noticed that the people on the floor above ours, the top floor, had left the door propped open. I knew from the incessant hammering and drilling we had been hearing all day long that the top floor was under construction, and I thought, *Maybe I'll just take a quick look and see how it's going.*

I had only intended to peek in through the open door, but I found myself passing the threshold to get a good look at the place. It was an exact replica of our office but completely blank, like someone had Ctrl + A, Deleted the desks, chairs, and cardboard cutout of Ryan Gosling. I quickly figured out the source of the cold wind: a window had been left open, and the brisk March air was pouring in. When I went to close it, I saw that, unlike the windows on our floor, this one had a roof right outside like a terrace. I thought, *Well, I'm already up here.* I opened the window wider, lay on my belly, and shimmied through.

It's a rare thing, being alone on a rooftop in Manhattan at night. The muffled sounds of the city radiated up from below, swirling in with the wind. I could see the Flatiron

Building sitting just up the street, Freedom Tower gleaming in the distance, and—oh my god—the Empire State Building just ten blocks away, dominating the sky to the north.

I walked to the ledge and felt my eyes well up—a combination of the whiskey, the cold wind, and the embarrassing rush of emotion I feel whenever my life resembles a scene from a movie. I peeked down at the street below and watched the late-night commuters shuffle down Twenty-Third Street in messy lines like picnic ants. I imagined hands clutching collars to throats and jammed in pockets, and the people they belonged to having no idea they were extras on my movie set.

But mostly I just stared at the Empire State Building, a structure I grew up trying to glimpse from high points in my suburban hometown. Usually I could only see the red tip of her spire: tiny and slight and invisible to the untrained eye, I quickly learned from trying to point it out to visitors. Tonight, though, she was tall enough to scrape the moon and close enough that her brilliant white lights glinted off the zipper of my coat.

Of course, I took about a million selfies.

I didn't want to leave, but I knew I'd already pushed my luck by going onto the roof in the first place. So after doing a 360-degree spin to take it all in and snapping another few pics to remember the night by, I left. I lowered the window to the height I'd found it at, slipped through the propped-open door, and took the stairs down to the lobby. On my way out I wished a bored security guard a pleasant evening and got on the N train back to Queens.

I woke up Saturday with a very big headache. I groaned, and Sean rolled over.

"Good morning," he said, groggy and half-asleep.

"Is it good?" I said, trying to massage away a sharp pain above my right eye.

"Where were you last night?" he asked.

"I drank an irresponsible amount of whiskey and snuck onto the roof of my office building," I said.

Sean picked his head up from the pillow and studied me with his one open eye. "I know one of those things is true."

I grabbed my phone off the nightstand and showed him the pictures. Even with sober eyes they looked amazing. The Empire State Building, glowing and massive, filled up the entire screen.

"Whoa, take me?"

"No way," I said, shoving my head under a pillow.

Sean lifted the pillow at the corner. "Why not?"

"Because it's probably illegal!" I said. "Breaking and entering or trespassing or being sneaky at your job."

"It's only illegal if you get caught," Sean countered.

"It was a mistake," I said, pulling the pillow back down. "And I'm never making it again."

As the hangover waned, a delayed paranoia took over. I had assumed that I had gotten away with my rooftop escapade when I said goodnight to the security guard and he didn't immediately ask if I was the person he'd just seen sneak into a private construction site on the security camera monitors. But then I started wondering if it was common practice to review all the weekend security footage on Monday morning. Sean assured me that was crazy. No one had the time or the bandwidth to review sixty hours of security footage just for good measure.

"But what if there was an incident? And something went missing? *Then* they'd review the tapes. And I'd be the only one up there," I said, taking a sip out of Sean's coffee mug like I did every morning.

"Okay, fine, in the unlikely event the top floor of your building was the target of a heist over the weekend, you might have a problem," Sean said, taking his steaming mug back from me.

I knew I was probably overreacting, but to be fair, my suspicions weren't completely unfounded. The first week we moved into the building, there had been a murder-suicide in the Home Depot on the first floor. Nearly a year after we moved out of the building, the Chelsea Bombings happened only one block to the west. And just a few days earlier I'd had forty dollars and a souvenir Brazilian real stolen out of my wallet by a stranger who found it flopped open in the lobby. This was New York! Bad things happened all the time.

My regret about the late-night roof romp swelled as Monday drew closer. Sunday night I tossed and turned, wondering if I should delete the photos—the *evidence*—off my phone. I didn't, acknowledging the fact that if you do epic shit and you don't have the selfies to prove it, it basically didn't even happen. The next morning, I walked down Twenty-Third Street glancing ahead to see if there was a police barricade outside my building. There wasn't, but I did mistake a halal food cart for a news van and almost swallowed my gum. When I got to my building, I tapped my ID at the security booth in the lobby and half-expected the guard to leap over the counter and apprehend me. He didn't even look up from his phone. I took the elevators up to the office and slunk to my desk. I avoided eye contact with coworkers, awash with the feeling that I'd done something weird in our shared home.

I spent the day flipping between writing a post and compulsively checking my email every four minutes. I was jumpy and on edge, and every bolded new message in my inbox made the breath catch in my throat. Would they just write "You're fired" in the subject line, or would they ease into it with something like "Roof?????"? I figured if I was going to get in trouble, it would come from my editor-in-chief, Ben. I was twenty-five years old and I still thought of my boss as an elementary school principal whose only job was to keep order in the newsroom and tell us we're doing a great job. But eventually six o'clock rolled around and my inbox never received an email from Ben, or the police, or the United States secretary of defense.

Back at home, I told Sean about my stressful day over dinner, which we ate sitting cross-legged around the coffee table in the living room. We had been fortunate enough to find an apartment with a real, live dining room—an entire room for dining! Before signing our lease, we assumed dining rooms were a New York City myth, like mole people or the subway timetable. We had been blessed with incredible fortune—and yet we still chose to eat every meal sitting like kindergarteners at circle time. As I talked, I flapped my knees up and down like a nervous butterfly.

"I think I'm in the clear," I told Sean. "Like, if nothing happened today, I think I'm good to go."

"Erin, you were never not in the clear. You are freaking out."

"I mean, I know that now. But I couldn't assume that until I officially made it to the clear, you know?"

"Sure," said Sean. "Whatever calms you down."

A few days went by, and I stopped thinking about the illegal roof jaunt entirely. Sean was right. I had been freaking out. What did I think they were going to do, arrest me? It's not like there were *signs*. I didn't jump over barriers that read: "Keep out or go to lady prison and ruin your entire future!" I walked through an *open* door. And then I shimmied like a snake through a slightly smaller but technically still *open* window. If they didn't want me to go out there, why had they basically put out welcome mats for me?

I shook my head and went back to writing a post about the weirdest objects people had stuck up their own butts. It was Wednesday, which meant free lunch at BuzzFeed. And it was the first, which meant free cupcakes in honor of everyone born that month. Plenty of stuff to look forward to.

At 11:32 I received an email from my manager, Tanner.

Subject: Do you have a minute?
Body: I'm in Harry Potter.

I emailed him back immediately: "Sure!!!!! Be there in a sec."

I figured Tanner wanted to meet with me about performance reviews, a protocol I'd managed to mess up every year that I'd worked at the company. Tanner was my manager (or my *Tanager*, as I liked to call him), but we were close, and sometimes these "meetings" were an excuse to hang out and chat for a quick five minutes.

I half-ran half-walked to the break-out room we called Harry Potter and shut the door behind me. Tanner stood with his back to the door, looking out the window.

"What's up?" I asked, taking a seat at the round table in the middle of the room.

Tanner turned around. "What'd you do Friday night?"

I felt my butt clench so tightly it could have cracked a walnut.

"I—why?" I asked.

"Security is investigating footage of someone going up on the roof, and they think it's you," Tanner said.

I stared at him.

"I saw the tapes," he said. "You can try denying it, but it would be easier for you to just comply with security."

Once, when I was thirteen years old, I was playing in a softball tournament with my club team and got behind in the count after watching a perfect pitch tear right through the strike zone. I said the word "fuck" to myself, and the umpire tapped me on the shoulder and said, "Young lady, if you say that word again I will throw you out of this game." The rush of shame and embarrassment was so intense that I literally felt hot and, for a second, thought I had peed my pants right there at home plate. That was the last time I felt that, the so-embarrassed-I'm-hot-and-maybe-peeing sensation, until this moment, twelve years later, sitting in a room called Harry Potter in front of a coworker who once respected me.

"I'm sorry," I said, because it was the only thing to say.

"Listen, *we* don't care. You're not in trouble with Buzz-Feed. But security needs you to sign something admitting it was you, and they'll tell you what the next steps are."

"OK," I said, standing up, wobbly-legged and suddenly shivering. I'd never been in trouble as an adult. I'd never even gotten a speeding ticket. The GIF of SpongeBob whimpering and cry-yelling, "But I'm a good noodle!" played over and over in my head as I made my way to the door.

Tanner cleared his throat. "Just go to the front desk in the lobby. They'll tell you what you need to do."

I nodded without turning around, took a deep breath, and left.

I walked to the elevator with my eyes glued to the floor, too scared that I might make eye contact with a coworker and they would instantly know upon meeting my glance that I was a dirty criminal. I imagined they'd splash their hot coffee in my face and hiss a weird insult like, "Why don't you go live on the roof, roof girl?"

I had made it all the way to the elevator without having to interact with anyone, but as the doors closed my coworker Lauren slipped in beside me. I stopped pressing the wall directly next to the DOOR OPEN button and managed a small hello.

"Hey!" she said. "Whoa, are you OK?"

"Yep! Fine!" I forced a smile so hard my teeth ached.

"Oh . . . OK. It's just, you look kind of . . . weird and pale," she said.

"Well, I might be going to jail right now," I said, still smiling.

"What the f—"

The elevator doors opened. I stepped out first. And there, in the lobby, was Sean.

"What are you DOING HERE?" I yelled, running over to him. "I'm in so much trouble. They found out about the roof. I'm so glad you're here. Wait, why are you here?"

"April Fools," he said.

I paused. Showing up at my job in the middle of the day unannounced had to be the worst prank in the history of tomfoolery, but I had no time to make fun of him for it.

"Great prank, Sean! But I can't talk right now because I have to go to jail for sneaking onto the roof," I said, pushing past him to get to the front desk.

Sean grabbed my arm. "No, Erin," he said. *"April Fools."*

And suddenly, it clicked. I wasn't in trouble. They didn't know about the roof. *All of this* was a prank. I looked at Sean and felt a relief so sweet I almost had to sit right down on the ground. Instead I shoved him backward until he tripped over and fell onto a couch.

"Are you mad?" he said, giggling.

"No, I'm SO RELIEVED," I said, diving on the couch next to him to catch my breath.

Sean reached into his backpack and pulled out a box of cupcakes. "OK, well, I bought you these in case you *were* mad. But since you're not, I guess I'll just keep them?"

"I'm mad, I'm so mad!" I yelled, grabbing the box from him. "How did you? When did you? So Tanner—?"

"Was in on it," Sean said.

"What the *hell*? Damn, you think you know someone. DAMN, he should really consider becoming an actor—"

Suddenly a security guard materialized in front of us. "Would you two please keep it down? This is a place of business."

I hid behind Sean's shoulder, still terrified I might still somehow end up in jail.

"Sorry," I heard him say. "We'll stop."

So that's my only dating advice. Find a carrot who understands your anxieties well enough to execute a prank so perfect you almost soil yourself in front of a coworker. Bonus points if he brings you cupcakes after.

WHY I CAN NEVER VISIT EGYPT

I've had my period over a hundred times in my life, and still every time it comes I think to myself, I can't believe this is an actual thing that happens. It's like the uterus is a magical storm cloud that lives inside your body and rains blood for days and days on end. How is everyone so calm about this?

Sometimes when I want to feel crazy I imagine a world that's exactly like ours in every single way except for one tiny difference: periods don't exist. I picture myself walking up to an unsuspecting inhabitant of this alternate universe and saying to them, "Every twenty-eight days my vagina discharges blood and uterine lining for the better part of a week and I can't stop it from happening." And then they start screaming, "HOW ARE YOU ALIVE?! SOMEONE GET THIS WOMAN TO A HOSPITAL BECAUSE SHE

SHOULD BE DEAD BY ALL ACCOUNTS. WHAT AN EXTRAORDINARY AND STRONG PERSON YOU MUST BE TO DEAL WITH THIS HELLISH AFFLICTION."

Growing up, periods eluded me, first in concept and then in initial arrival. When I was in third grade I became vaguely aware women had periods, but I assumed periods had something to do with pyramids because the words were so similar. I imagined a tiny, spinning pyramid deep inside a woman's belly, but how it got there and how long it stayed I could not figure out. Then one day my sister's friend Elinor mentioned that she read a story in *YM* magazine where a girl got her period in the middle of the night but forgot to change her sheets and after school her crush came over and saw the blood and isn't that *so* embarrassing? In what may be the single most uncool moment of my entire life, I responded by clapping my hands over my ears and screaming, "BLOOD?!"

"Uh, yeah," she said, looking at me as if she could actually see the four-year age difference between us. "What d'you think a period *is*?"

In that moment I accepted that the world is a chaotic and terrifying hellscape, and I should never, ever visit Egypt.

By the time I got to middle school, though, I had a pretty firm grasp on the concept of periods. After all, I had

watched the cringey puberty video in fifth grade, where
dancing maxi pads sang about the virtues of proper hygiene.
And my mom had yelled The Talk at me when we were
alone in the car on the way to ShopRite, as if puberty was a
thing I had caused by being careless.

"You're going to start growing hair on your yingyang
and bleeding from it once a month, OK?!" she yelled at the
windshield, knuckles white on the steering wheel.

"OK! OK! I'm sorry! Please slow down!"

Despite that comprehensive sex education, there still
remained a few tiny details with which I still struggled. Like
flow, for example. Did it just drip out of you like a leaky fau-
cet or did it happen in powerful bursts like a Super Soaker?

I sometimes tried to sneak these questions in while
talking on the phone with my friend Jessi, who had gotten
her period right before we graduated elementary school. It
was arguably the best time to get it—before everyone else,
but not so early that people's parents start speculating about
the hormone levels in dairy products.

"What does it feel like?" I asked her once, feigning
nonchalance.

"Oh," Jessi sighed into the phone, sounding like a world-
weary woman of twelve long years. "It's awful. It makes
your bones feel heavy."

I sat back in my inflatable armchair and tried to imagine how it must feel to be pinned down by the weight of one's own womanhood.

But then the months went by, and one by one my friends started getting their periods. Suddenly Jessi wasn't the odd woman out for having hers; I was the odd one for not having mine. I looked around the lunch table at my friends and felt like they had all been abducted by the same alien. It didn't matter how many times I heard "My mom cried!" and "My dad bought me flowers!" I would never understand what they had gone through until the glowing green light came for me, too.

It wasn't just their periods, though. My friends all started changing in other ways. Suddenly everyone cared about clothes and makeup, like the alien had made them read through old issues of *Vogue* in the spaceship waiting room while they prepared to have the period chip implanted. I tried my best to assimilate: I wore white eyeliner for about a week before I decided it made me look like I'd tried eating powdered doughnuts with my eyes, and I used all of my birthday money to buy a single tank top at Hollister even though it had holes in it. Still, I always felt a little bit like I didn't quite get it, like fashion was a test I kept failing.

Luckily my friends were eager to help me catch up. I remember during one lunchtime, a girl named Sam, whose mom let her get highlights in her already blond hair, ripped a sheet of notebook paper out of her Trapper Keeper and drew some rotating *C*'s on it.

"What logo is this?" Sam asked, tapping the paper with her purple gel pen.

"Coach," I said. Easy. Most of the girls at my school had a Coach wristlet where they kept their lunch money, a Burt's Bees lip balm, and, if they were *that* kind of wealthy, a Nokia cell phone.

"Yes!" Sam said. She pulled the paper back toward her and drew two interlocking *F*'s.

"OK, how about this?" she said, pushing the paper back over to me.

"Um, Ferrari?"

"Ew, like the car? No, no, no. Fendi," Sam said, writing the word under the logo in microscopic, perfect print. She twisted her mouth to one side. "You know what? I'm just going to make you a guide you can study with all the important designers on it. I'll quiz you tomorrow."

Sam bent over the paper and began drawing *LV*'s, overlapping *C*'s, and double *G*'s. I pretended to see a friend across the lunchroom and got out of there fast.

I quickly decided none of that mattered, anyway. Getting older had little to do with Coach bags and organic lip balm. I mean, my mom was old and she didn't have a designer bag. She kept her belongings in the chest pocket of her overalls, where they were safe from theft yet easy to access.

If I wanted to feel closer to my friends, I didn't need to dress like them; I just needed to get my goddamn period already. No one could deny I was just one of the girls if the proof was literally oozing out of me. And on a purely fundamental level, having my period would allow me to have something to say when my friends talked about *their* periods. And therefore bond with them, and therefore get invited to their sleepovers, and therefore restore order in our group. I could see myself now, lying tummy-down on a sleeping bag on the floor of my friend's den, kicking my feet back and forth in the air and saying, "Yes, Jennifer. I, too, find the cardboard applicators to be far inferior to the plastic ones. Ha, ha, ha. Isn't being a woman wonderful?"

These were trying times. For us un-perioded girls there was nothing to do but sit and wait for its arrival, but the waiting drove some people crazy. I heard a rumor that someone in our grade had gone through an entire box of tampons practicing her insert technique so she'd be ready when her first period came. Was *I* supposed to do that? I didn't have a box of tampons, but my parents kept a wicker basket of Q-tips on the back of the toilet. One evening I found myself pinching together Q-tips until the bundle reached a tampon-like girth. They were cotton, right? They were stick shaped, right? I held the bundle at eye level like I was staring down the barrel of a gun. *Am I going to do this?*

Without a second thought I returned the swabs to their basket and backed away from the toilet. "Keep it together, girl!" I whispered to myself through gritted teeth. I left the bathroom and went to my room to lie facedown on my bed and think about what I'd almost done.

I ended up getting my period on Valentine's Day in seventh grade at the Paramus Park Mall, and, no, the symbolism of reaching sexual maturity on a holiday dedicated to boning was not lost on me even then. I had gone with my older sister, Liz, to pick up candles for a romantic dinner she planned to make for her boyfriend in our parents' kitchen that night. Somewhere between the mall entrance and Yankee Candle, I stopped to use the bathroom, and when I pulled down my underwear (yellow briefs with a cartoon panda on the front that my mom had bought me from Limited Too), there in the crotch was a brownish-reddish mess.

When we made eye contact—me and the period—I was not overcome with a rush of maturity like I'd hoped. I didn't suddenly hear Shania Twain's "Man! I Feel Like a Woman" playing in my head or feel a maternal instinct toward the toddler whining two stalls over. Instead I thought with alarming clarity, *I'm going to have to deal with this every month for the next forty years*, and shoved a wad of toilet paper in my ruined underwear as a makeshift pad. When I rejoined Liz in the hallway, I didn't say a word to her. But in my head all I kept thinking was that I had entered the Paramus Park Mall a girl and would leave it a woman.

Things didn't change when I got back to school. Eventually I would figure out that the separation I felt from my friends wasn't biological, it was just middle school. People were growing and forming new interests and that meant realigning friend groups. I would eventually settle into a group that fluctuated over the next six years until graduation scattered us into a dozen different directions, periods notwithstanding.

I wish I could say my period and I lived happily ever after, that the struggles of menstrual ineptitude died in seventh grade alongside my center part and puka shell necklace. Things were pretty smooth sailing on the Red Sea for about six years. But when I had cancer, my oncologist medically induced me into temporary menopause in an attempt to preserve my fertility during chemo. Last to menstruate, first to stop.

"So this will protect my eggs from the chemo drugs?" I asked him while sitting on the paper-covered table in his examination room.

"Well, we don't know that for sure. But it's worth a shot!" he said, as he plunged the needle into the fat of my arm.

(This, by the way, is a common sentiment in cancer treatment. I had two CT scans before the technician started laying a pillow over my chest on my way into the machine.

"What is this for?" I asked. "They've never done this before."

"It's to protect your breast tissue from radiation."

"A pillow will protect my breast tissue from radiation?"

"A pillow won't *not* protect your breast tissue from radiation!"

A few weeks after the first shot my period came to a grinding halt. I stopped bleeding, PMSing, and cramping entirely.

"We're *so* jealous," my sisters told me.

"That's a funny thing to say to a person with cancer," I said back.

The truth was I hated not getting my period. It was just another thing cancer had taken from me, along with my hair, my health, and my ability to digest spicy foods. So when my period finally returned in a rush of blood and emotions nearly twelve months later, I welcomed it with open arms. *I'll never take you for granted, you beautiful, horrible liquid alarm clock*, I thought as I ran to CVS to buy tampons for the first time in so long that I forgot which aisle they were stocked in. *I'll always cherish you.*

So maybe that's what I thought I was doing when I bought my first menstrual cup. "Cherishing" my period.

A menstrual cup, for those who don't stay abreast of the hottest period trends, is a small, soft, silicon receptacle you insert into the vagina to catch blood for up to twelve hours before removing, dumping, and reinserting. The cup is shaped like a miniature wine glass but with a very short stem and no base (when the cup is full, the resemblance is uncanny). Menstrual cups are great because they eliminate waste and save money, as one cup can be used for years on end. They also alleviate the need to tote around a purse full of tampons, which was exciting news for me, a woman who owns zero purses.

The cup had been the suggestion of my best friend, Alijah. She had switched months earlier and swore she would never turn back to the dark world of cotton-based feminine products. She was a free woman! A born-again menstruater! And all it would take for me to join her was thirty dollars and an Amazon account.

I was intrigued. Especially because once a month I'd receive a Snapchat from Alijah of her sanitizing her cup in a pot of boiling water with captions like "Soup's on!" and "Mama's makin' a brew!" I liked the idea that I, too, could act like a creepy witch in my own kitchen. But even more than that, I liked that I could lessen my impact on the environment, that there would be fewer sea turtles choking on used tampons in our planet's oceans thanks to me and my righteous vagina. I'd be ahead of my time, a champion of herstory. Plus, I'd save about eight bucks a month, which, when you think about it, is around the price of a Chipotle burrito. Saving the environment *and* a free burrito? Sign me the fuck up.

I logged onto Amazon and purchased one menstrual cup and one used copy of Sylvia Plath's *The Bell Jar*. I figured if I was going to reinvent myself, femininely speaking, I might as well go balls deep.

The package arrived one Tuesday evening after work. I couldn't believe my luck: I happened to have my period, which meant I could start using it right away. I ran inside and

ripped open the box, tossing Plath to the side and presenting
Sean with the newest member of our family, Lil' Cup.

"Congratulations," he said. "I'm sure you two will have
many happy years together."

"Up to ten, according to this FAQ!" I said, pointing to
the side of the box.

Next I sent Alijah no fewer than thirteen Snaps of the
cup with captions like "CUP TWINS" and "TWO GIRLS,
ONE CUP (each)."

While I waited for her response, I read the directions insert front and back. It seemed pretty simple: Step
one, fold the cup into a C shape for easy insertion. Step two,
insert. Step three, remove when full by pulling on the short
silicon stem (this, it seemed, would be the only tricky part,
since unlike a tampon, the ripcord stayed tucked inside the
body and not dangling outside of it). Step four, luxuriate in
menstrual bliss like the modern woman you are!

"Wish me luck!" I yelled to Sean before slamming the
bathroom door.

It only took me two tries to get the fold right, and
before long I had successfully inserted the cup. *That wasn't
bad at all!* I thought. I had read so much on the Internet
about there being a steep learning curve with menstrual
cups. "Don't get discouraged if you don't get it the first

time!" the lifestyle bloggers urged. Clearly those pep talks were for women who had less practice shoving things into their secret compartment. I, on the other hand, had been using applicator-less tampons since middle school, a fact that earned me much deference in the P.E. locker room. I was practically *born* for the cup. I couldn't believe I had lived twenty-four years without it.

I emerged from the bathroom like I was walking onto a Broadway stage.

"It's in," I announced, taking a deep bow.

"Wow, I'm having flashbacks to high school," Sean said from the couch.

"Well, off to bed!" I said, prancing toward the bedroom.

"You can leave it in overnight?" he called after me.

I pranced back into the living room. "Twelve whole hours, which is four hours longer than a tampon, which means I can sleep as long as I want. This is already the best decision I've ever made. See you in the morning!" I kissed Sean goodnight and then bent over, cupped my hands around my belly, and addressed the cup directly. "And I'll see *you* in the morning, too!"

I awoke the next day around eight A.M. and zoomed into the bathroom, excited to see what my cup had harvested while

I slept. I consulted the directions insert one more time before attempting to remove the cup. There was a lot of talk of "bearing down" and using your pelvic floor muscles to force the cup out, which I had missed the night before on my initial perusal. But the rest seemed pretty intuitive. Grip the stem and pull down. Simple enough.

I tried first sitting on the toilet, which was listed under Approved Cup Removal Positions. Immediately I noticed that the cup had sort of shifted in my sleep and sat now at a jaunty angle; the stem no longer pointed straight down toward the floor, but at a slant, like it was pointing at my left ankle. I could just barely pinch the stem, but when I pulled down my fingers slid off and the cup stayed firmly put. I tried again with my left hand, thinking I'd get a better angle on it, but the same thing happened.

This is fine, I thought. I knew Alijah removed her cup in the shower because she said it always reminded her of the scene from *Psycho* and I could never shake the image. That was probably the best method for me, too, I figured. We're best friends, after all! It made sense we'd have the same menstrual cup removal position.

I hopped up from the toilet and started the shower running. Once inside, I tried removing the cup standing. Then squatting. Then with one leg on the ledge of the tub.

After ten or so tries I shut off the water and just stood there, dripping and wide-eyed, until I started to shiver.

A knock on the bathroom door startled me back to reality.

"Hey, can I, like, use the bathroom?" When I didn't answer, Sean opened the door.

"Whoa, hello, Samara. Are you OK?" he asked when he saw me.

"It's stuck."

"What?"

"The cup. It's stuck. I can't get it out."

"Really? Did you read the directions?"

"*Yes*, I read the directions. I can reach it but I can't yank it out!"

"OK. Are you sure you're not—I don't know—clenching? Your eyebrows are, like, four inches higher than they normally are. You seem tense. Maybe your vagina is also tense?"

"Yeah, I am tense. I have an object stuck inside my body."

"OK. Well. Did you text Alijah?"

"Good idea!" I said as I sprang out of the shower and pushed past Sean, leaving a trail of wet footprints in my wake. I grabbed my phone off the kitchen counter and texted Alijah, my thumbs moving so fast they became blurs.

ME: Lij, the cup is stuck!! I can reach it but I can't get a good enough grip to pull it out. Help!!!!!

While I waited for a response, I tapped my phone against my chin and imagined how I'd phrase this to the receptionist at my gynecologist's office. And then I imagined how I'd phrase this to the guy writing my obituary because I was way too embarrassed to call my gynecologist.

My phone buzzed.

ALIJAH: Yeah, that'll happen. Did you try bearing down?

ME: Literally what does that mean!!

ALIJAH: Just pretend you're giving birth to it!

ME: Oh, easy enough. I'll just do what I did all those other times I gave birth?!

ALIJAH: Haha. True.

ME: Well?? What do I do????

ALIJAH: Try and relax! Deep breaths! And then just like reaaaaally push.

ALIJAH: PUSH ERIN PUSH

ALIJAH: Hee hee hoo hee hee hoo

Back in the bathroom, I sat on the toilet and took a deep breath, eyes closed. *You're in a delivery room*, I told myself. *You're about to give birth to your tiny, cup-shaped son. The shampoo bottles are your friends and family. The sink is your OB-GYN.*

Then, on the count of three, I pushed as hard as I could, until my face turned red and the pressure in my head made my temples hurt. I checked if the cup had lowered at all. Nope. Still up there.

ME: It's not working.

ALIJAH: Are you calm? I feel like you're not calm. Are you sure you're not clenching?

ME: Why does everyone keep saying that!!

At this point, there were two things more pressing than the actual cup itself: First, I was running late for work and would either have to call in sick or go in with the cup stuck inside me. And second, I had just passed the thirteen-hour mark, which is around the time the directions recommend seeking medical attention.

Defeated, I trudged back into the living room.

"Well," I said, readjusting my towel. "I'm going to die."

"Still stuck up there, eh?" Sean ate a spoonful of cereal without looking up from the TV.

I sat down next to him on the couch.

"Sean," I said.

"Yeah," he said, still looking at the TV.

"Would you be interested in going on a rescue mission for a missing POW?" I asked.

Sean placed his bowl on the coffee table and turned toward me, placing a hand on my knee.

"I love you," he said. "But this is one journey you have to go on alone."

I sighed. "The box says I have to go to the hospital now."

"Are you gonna?"

"No," I said. "I'd rather die."

"OK," he said, picking his cereal bowl back up. "Then you better tell work."

I slid off the couch, making theatrical, sad noises. I grabbed my phone off the counter and started drafting an email to our editorial director.

Hi Jack. Please excuse my lateness today, I have a menstrual cup lodged inside my vaginal canal . . .

Delete.

Jacky, it's Chacky!!! Do you know what a menstrual cup is? Haha, well Google it and listen to this . . .

Delete. Delete.

Jack—Something came up, I'll be working from home
until further notice!

Send.

I went back into the bathroom to give the cup another
go. Standing in front of the toilet I tried hopping up and
down and massaging my belly to help loosen the cup or
calm myself down or both. Then I opened the medicine
cabinet in search of a tool that could assist in the extraction
process. Floss? No. Although I loved the idea of lassoing
it out like a cowboy. Toothbrushes? Well, maybe if I held
them like chopsticks and . . . No, the problem wasn't reaching the cup, it was getting a good enough grip. I needed
pliers or vice grips or . . . tweezers! My fumbling weak
fingers were no match for my strong vaginal clutches, but
maybe tweezers could do the job. I doused the tweezers
in rubbing alcohol to kill any lingering eyebrow germs and
dried them with a square of toilet paper. Then, with one
foot planted on the toilet, I brought the tweezers between
my legs.

It only took a second of the pointy, cold metal coming
into contact with my labia for me to realize no, no, fuck no,
no, this will not work. I slammed the tweezers down on the

sink and left the bathroom to lay my head in Sean's lap and whimper like a stray dog.

We watched bad morning TV in our underwear and ate bowls of Frosted Mini-Wheats while hour fourteen came and went. I started to calm down, even as facts about toxic shock syndrome rocketed into my brain. This was a part of being an adult that I did not foresee when I was younger—that some days you have to blow off work to watch *Live with Kelly* because you got an object stuck in your own lady tunnel.

During a commercial break I decided to give the cup another shot.

"Are you going to try again?" Sean asked.

"Yeah, I mean, I gotta get it out!" I said, wheeling around and throwing my hands into the air.

"Hey," he said. "Eyebrows."

I relaxed my face and felt my eyebrows returning to their normal position for the first time all morning.

In the bathroom, I tried not to focus on how long the cup had been inside of me but on how free I felt now that I didn't have to rush to work. I took an actual deep breath and sang "Twinkle, Twinkle, Little Star" to myself. With my finger and thumb on the stem I tried wiggling the cup back and forth again. At first the cup didn't budge, but I stayed calm, relaxing every muscle in my body, including the ones that controlled my eyebrows, and started singing louder. I had all day, after all. Then, something clicked in my head. Bearing down didn't mean tensing all your muscles and forcing the cup out. It meant engaging the abdominal muscles and opening the pelvic ones. I felt like a cavewoman relying on instinct to deliver a cavechild alone in the middle of the lion-infested wilderness. I was doing it! The cup was wiggling free!

Finally, I had managed to get it low enough to grip around the base. With one sure yank the cup popped out. I couldn't believe it. Free! At last! I held the cup at eye level and felt exactly how Sir Arthur must have felt the day he pulled the sword from the stone. Victorious. Triumphant. Covered in blood.

"SEAN!" I yelled. "I DID IT, I GOT IT OUT!"

"Nice," he yelled through the door. "Did the eyebrow thing work?"

"Shut up!" I yelled. "This is my moment, don't try and take it!"

I stood there for a minute or two more basking in my feminine victory, feeling the warm rays of Aphrodite shining down on me, before I realized there was nothing left to do but pop that sucker back in and get to work.

On my way to the train, I texted Alijah a flurry of messages.

ME: I fucking DID IT dude! It took all morning but I BIRTHED that thing. It was like once I relaxed my body knew what to do and took over

ME: It was so fucking NATURAL I am JUICED on being a woman right now.

ALIJAH: That's my girl!!! Knew u could do it

ME: I LOVE VAGINAS. Do you think I should make a shirt that says that?

ALIJAH: I want one too!!

GREENER PASTURES

My therapist is tired of talking about *The Fault in Our Stars*. She specializes in cancer survivorship and bereavement, which means a lot of the conversations she has with her patients go like this: You are not Hazel Grace. There is no Augustus Waters. This is not *The Fault in Our Stars*. OK?

She's never had to have that talk with me, though. I am the middle child of my family, and I know better than to expect anything from the universe.

"You know," she told me once, "most of my patients ask me, 'Why me?' You're the first person who's ever said, 'Why *not* me?'"

"Well, who the fuck am I?" I said.

As I explained to my therapist, I've come to think about it like this: Cancer is an act of nature. Nature is chaotic and uncalculating. When a tornado rips down an open field, it doesn't sidestep for a farmhouse. Why should I feel victimized that cancer didn't sidestep for me?

I don't blame cancer, but I also don't blame my therapist for being frustrated with the version of cancer we see in books and movies. In *The Fault in Our Stars*, cancer comes with a lot of accessories. Romance! Travel! Handsome one-legged boys! It makes sense that people who read the book before getting diagnosed might feel a little cheated when all they get is a shiny, bald head and a free can of ginger ale. Because the thing about cancer, the thing about most things, is that it's actually pretty boring in real life. You spend half the time in waiting rooms and the other half waiting to go into waiting rooms. You sleep a lot. You watch a lot of TV. It's dull and unsexy, even the groin exams.

I read *The Fault in Our Stars* a few years after it became popular, after seeing the black-and-white illustrated clouds take over my Tumblr feed. At that point, I had been cancer-free for about five years, which felt like a healthy emotional distance from the experience, and had seen a coworker stuff a copy into her tote bag as we walked out of work one evening. I asked, "Hey, is that any good? I'm thinking about reading it." She looked at me like one might look at a child who asked for a sip of Daddy's beer. "It's good, but I don't know if you should read it. It's, like, probably pretty trig-gering for someone like you." I ordered a copy on my phone before our elevator hit the ground floor.

For those uninitiated, *The Fault in Our Stars* is narrat-ed from the perspective of a seventeen-year-old girl named Hazel Grace who has a terminal form of thyroid cancer. She meets a boy, Augustus, in her cancer support group who has been cancer-free since the amputation of his leg. Hazel likes Augustus (because he is movie star handsome and peanut butter smooth), but she knows she shouldn't start a rela-tionship with him since her cancer is so touch and go. They fall in love anyway.

I very much enjoyed the book. And no, it didn't trigger me. (A note to my coworkers: If you think I don't think about death, I regret to inform you that my brain is just me imagin-ing my own funeral and the jingle for Kars4Kids on a constant, never-ending loop.) I thought the book was a fair portrayal of what it's like to be a teenager with cancer, just like I think *The Lord of the Rings* is a fair portrayal of what it's like to be a hobbit with magical jewelry. It was a lovely sidestep from reality, and I liked the journey as much as any-one with a pulse would.

I saw John Green once when he came to BuzzFeed to be interviewed for a profile. I can always tell how beloved a celebrity guest is by counting how many BuzzFeed employees pretend to make coffee when he or she visits. The way the office is set up, it's easiest to catch a glimpse of the person by taking a long, ambling route to the canteen. A lot of people made coffee that day.

I sat in my chair and unabashedly swiveled 180 degrees to watch him cross the office. A pack of my coworkers lingered a few paces behind him with their favorite John Green books tucked under their arms. It made me proud as an aspiring writer to see him drawing the same enthusiasm as rappers and models. It made me even prouder as an ex-cancer teen to see most of the books jammed in my coworkers' armpits were copies of *The Fault in Our Stars*.

Obviously there are a few key differences between my story and the novel. I didn't go to Amsterdam and eat a three-course meal at a five-star restaurant overlooking a world-famous canal. I did, however, go to New York in my mom's van and eat matzo ball soup at a diner on Sixty-Second Street while I waited to be called for treatment. I didn't fall in love with a death-obsessed, fast-talking man-teen. Instead, I stayed in love with a boy who sometimes pronounces foliage "foilage." I didn't meet a world-famous author, but I did get to hang out with some truly top-notch nurses (shout out to Fatima, a woman who could find a vein on a burned-up corpse in an alleyway). My experience was like *The Fault in Our Stars* if someone turned the dial from eleven down to two or three. The bargain-brand: *The Flaw in Our Balls of Gas*.

Sure, there were some notable moments during my cancer experience—not *The Fault in Our Stars*–level moments, but slightly less boring moments than the rest. The most romantic, teenagey thing I did that year was on the eve of my twentieth birthday. I had driven to Sean's college in the Bronx and was hanging out in his apartment when his roommate, Brian, handed me an unopened carton of expired orange juice.

"Why are you giving this to me?" I asked, confused, tired, and bald.

"I think you should throw it out the window," Brian said, as he crossed the room to open the screen.

"Why?" I said, still confused (and tired and bald).

"Because it's your last day being a teenager and nothing matters," he said gesturing toward the now open window.

I'm generally against this type of hedonist abandonment. When people throw caution to the wind, I am stuck imagining the poor soul who has to break his back sweeping caution into a dustpan (and usually in my mind it's a hard-working janitor with a heart of gold and a push-broom mustache). I can't even shell peanuts directly onto the floor of Yankee Stadium without feeling guilty, and that's half the point of seeing a ball game. But Brian was making a compelling argument, and I was technically a guest in his beer-scented, sticky-floored home.

I stood up from Sean's bed and walked over to the window. I looked back at Sean, who seemed to shrug with his entire body, as if tossing juice off buildings was a weird but obligatory rite of passage we all have to go through at some point. Then I underarm-hurled the carton through the open window and into the night sky, sending it soaring in a perfect arc down four stories before connecting with a stop sign below with a satisfying *DOOSH*.

Brian was right. Nothing matters.

Death doesn't matter either, I've come to believe. And that's the last striking difference between John Green's characters and me: no one in my story has died (yet). After going through all of this, I've come to realize that death doesn't matter to the person who died, it matters only to the people who remain. If things had gone sour for me, I would have died and gone back to that preplace I was before I was born. There would be no pain, emotional or otherwise, just a sleepy nothingness, an absence of life. But here on earth, there would be heartbreak and strife and Facebook posts and hashtags and memorials and emotional breakdowns in cars parked outside White Manna ("She loved those *fucking* burgers").

The truth is, surviving cancer doesn't *really* save your life, does it? It just postpones a death that is still coming. If things go well and you survive, you'll have the privilege of growing old and dying at a time that's more convenient for your friends and family, a time when people can shrug and say, "She lived a good life. Now let's eat some expensive Italian food and tell stories about her that make us laugh and cry."

While my relationship with death has always been weird, going through this whole cancer thing only made it more complicated. I had a strangely morbid childhood. My birthday is one week before Halloween, and as a kid I'd walk to school mentally preparing to turn a year older while passing paper ghosts hanging from trees and cardboard gravestones littering front lawns. My mom would often include one last-minute gift from the CVS seasonal aisle in my birthday pile, and when I turned eight I received a four-foot plastic skeleton with red eyes and a haunting grin. I named him Mr. Bones and played with him by tossing him down the playground slide or stuffing him into the tire swing and sending him on a ride. This remained a theme well into adulthood. When I turned twenty-one, my mom presented me with a chocolate cake in the shape of a coffin. White icing spelled out RIP on one side and black plastic spiders were scattered on the top.

"Jesus Christ, Mom," my older sister, Liz, said. "She hasn't even been in remission for a full year."

"What?" my mom said. "She's my little Halloween baby!"

By middle school I had accepted that death is more than a decoration; it's a thing that happens to pets, relatives I have never met, and bad guys in movies. Thanks to back-to-back sleepovers, I also became convinced that death was going to happen to me when the girl from *The Ring* and the clown from *It* teamed up to eat my face in the middle of the night. I slept on my parents' floor for a socially destructive length of time.

In high school death became even more real. By the time I graduated I had lost all four grandparents, countless friends' parents and siblings, and a handful of classmates. People died so frequently that sophomore year I invested in a pair of funeral slacks to minimize the inevitable grief-fueled freak-out over what to wear when someone I knew died. Suddenly monsters from horror movies seemed a lot less threatening than driving a little too fast down a side street lined with telephone poles. There was no floor to sleep on to make that any less scary.

By the time I got cancer, it only seemed fair that it might kill me. Death had been circling me for years; if it didn't eventually catch up with me, I would have thought it was deliberately letting me win. Of course, I was still scared of dying and dealt with my fear by dissociating. Sean and I made an aggressively casual suicide pact: an if-you-go-down-I-go-down-with-you agreement, which shows, I think, my level of mental preparation. Neither of us expected him to follow through had it come to that. But I found it comforting to pretend I wouldn't have to do it alone, like he had kindly offered to come with me to the DMV, even though it's the worse place on earth.

When I got better, death lingered. Five months after I went into remission, my high school friend Meg told me that her mom, Jackie, was going into hospice. Jackie had been diagnosed with lung cancer around the same time I was diagnosed with Hodgkin's. It had been fun at first. We shaved our heads around the same time, and Jackie threw a barbecue to show off our new 'dos. When I showed up she was standing on the deck holding an iced tea, and she screamed across the party, "Look at you, you little bald babe! You look like a supermodel, for Christ's sake. Get up here!" But as the months wore on and I began to recover, she had gotten worse.

I went over to visit Meg and Jackie as soon as I found out. All of the furniture in the living room had been shoved into a corner to make room for a large mechanical hospital bed in the center, where a tiny version of Jackie lay silently. I stood by Jackie's side and petted her bald head while Meg explained from the other side of the bed that at this point, they were really just waiting. Jackie had become paralyzed from the neck down from tumors that spread to her spine and couldn't do more than roll her eyes and groan. I looked at her, hollow and sunken, tiny and frail. She had been a beautiful, tall, loud redheaded woman with piercing blue eyes, and now all that remained were the eyes, which looked right through us as she struggled for breath. This is exactly where I could've been, I realized. This is exactly what I would've looked like, except that I don't even have nice eyes. I kissed Jackie on the temple and told Meg I'd come visit again next week. She died four days later.

These days I have lost the will to sugarcoat death. I have looked death in the eyes too many times to deny its existence, which is a thing I notice people do as often as they comment on the weather. I was riding the elevators up to the editorial floor at work one morning when my coworker Nathan remarked on my weekend bag.

"Going somewhere?" he asked, gesturing at my luggage with his cup of coffee.

"Nowhere special, just home to Jersey for a night," I said.

"Oh, that's right, you grew up nearby, right?"

"Not too far," I said. "About ten miles from the George Washington Bridge."

"Wow, that's wild to think," Nathan said, glancing up at the ceiling. "That you've been coming in and out of the city your whole life. When I moved here from Ohio my mom was like, 'Don't go to New York! You'll die!'"

I scrunched up my face. "You'd die if you stayed in Ohio, too. You're gonna die either way."

"That's . . . true, I guess," Nathan said.

"Hey, can we save the death talk till eleven, please? I haven't even had my coffee," someone called out from the back of the elevator.

"Yeah, it's a little early for me to be contemplating my mortality," another voice chimed in. And then everyone forced out a desperate laugh, as if the sound would scare away the death cloud I'd just conjured.

This, to me, is crazy. It's literally never too early in the day to talk about death. Death doesn't sleep! Not talking about dying doesn't protect you from it. Have all the coffee you want, Sheila from accounting. You're still going to die.

That may seem cavalier, or brave even, but it's not. People love to couple cancer survivors and bravery, but they get the relationship between them wrong: Cancer doesn't make you brave; it only helps you to see the depth of the bravery you've always had. Of course I still fear death like I'm programmed to do; I still hate when a crowded subway stops under the East River and when the fasten seatbelt light dings on airplanes. But what I've realized is that I'm more scared of losing someone I love than I am of losing myself. I'd rather put the killing thing between my own teeth than have to watch someone else bite down. Having cancer made me realize that.

It's weird, but I actually find great comfort in the fact that everything ends. It's the only fair part of life, really—that no one gets to stay. It doesn't matter how much money you make or how many friends you have; when the time comes, you gotta mosey on, partner. And it's sweet to think that most of us don't want to go, like life is a party that's too fun to leave. How lucky we are to even be invited.

By that same token, I don't believe Sean and I will be together forever, because I've accepted that forever doesn't exist outside fairy tales and pop songs. We will have to break up, either because we choose to or death chooses for us. Hazel Grace calls this a little infinity. I call it reality. And maybe that's why I find myself awake at night squinting through the darkness to check that Sean's chest is rising and falling.

Because while the thought scares me more than anything in the world, I accept that one day it won't.

URINE TROUBLE

I've only peed my pants once in my life, and it was 100 percent on my own terms. As a child I had very quickly made the connection that the kids who peed their pants were the same kids who cried when their moms dropped them off at school every day: aka Grade-A Babies. After watching a boy named Christopher in my preschool class pee his pants *while* crying for his mom, I made the decision that pants-peeing was not for me. It just seemed like such a childish thing to do, considering that we were already children. Come on, Christopher! You're a walking parody of yourself! Don't give the people what they expect!

It happened in kindergarten. I had already earned myself the reputation of DGAF Queen among my classmates for flooding the sand table during playtime. I had spent the first half hour building an imposing, multi-turreted sand fortress only to realize upon completion that if I expected it to survive any serious enemy attack, it needed a moat. So for the remaining half hour I took one of the tiny paper cups we used for snack time and, with the patience of a tightrope walker, inched back and forth from the bathroom to the sand table, filling and emptying cupfuls of water until the fortress was encircled by a mighty, flowing river of tap water.

When my teacher looked up from her temp work and saw what I had done, she screamed. At first I thought she was having the appropriate reaction anyone would have when presented with the world's most intimidating sand castle, but it turns out her reaction was a mixture of both rage and sadness that I had ruined the sand table, which, from what I now understand about public school budgets, was probably paid for out of her own pocket.

"ERIN. Why did you do this?" she demanded, redness filling the spaces between her freckles.

"To keep out bad guys," I said.

I got put in time-out, the first and last of my grade school career, and, while I sat and stared at the thickly painted cinder-block wall inches from my face, I thought about how strange it was that grown-ups punished kids for their great ideas.

After doing my time, word of my delinquency spread quickly around the classroom. I knew my classmates felt differently about me because, when playing house, I was no longer offered the role of Dog but Older Sister, which required me to sit in the corner of the play-kitchen and pretend a building block was a telephone that I talked on while ignoring my play-mom.

As life went on I became more comfortable in my new, alternative social status. I sat on the back of the carpet during circle time. I wore a lot of tank tops. I even started a play-fire in the play-kitchen (only two people play-died). And then one random Wednesday my teacher announced we'd be doing something special instead of playtime. I looked around the room to gauge everyone's reactions. Kids seemed pretty doubtful that anything could be more special than an hour of uninterrupted playtime, and I had to agree. I had plans to administer strep throat tests to all the plastic dinosaurs in the toy bin that day. But then she announced we'd be visiting the computer lab to practice typing, and cheers broke out throughout the classroom. A couple kids started chanting "Computers! Computers! Computers!" while banging their little fists on the grubby yellow tabletops. In the nineties there were few things more exciting than one-finger typing on a PC the size of a microwave oven. I had only touched

one other computer before, a boxy, beige thing in my friend
Dana's living room. We played a desktop game where
a pixelated baby tumbled out of an apartment building
window and you had to catch the baby in a net before it
hit the unforgiving 2-D ground. When my mom showed up
two hours later to take me home, I hid in the bathroom in
hopes that she would grow impatient and let me live there
forever.

Once our class calmed down, we lined up at the door in
a perfect single file, everyone too eager and anxious to delay
even a second of precious computer time. When the teacher
went to grab her workbag from her desk, I turned to a girl
named Kayla behind me. She was pale and yellow-haired
and had all of her fingers in her mouth at once. I noticed she
was trembling.

"What's wrong?" I asked.

Her translucent blue eyes focused on me. She removed
her soggy fingers to speak.

"I'm so excited," she whispered.

We left the classroom and followed the teacher through
the halls in the world's most obedient conga line. We were
silent except for the occasional unsuppressed wail of excite-
ment, followed by a chorus of shushes. Down the hallway we
marched, past the gym and up a staircase I had never used

before, until we were deposited in an unfamiliar wing on the second floor. Slowly I noticed a change in our surroundings; the walls were drained of their bright, happy colors and the bulletin boards were filled not with drawings but lines and lines of text. We were in the sixth grade hallway, I guessed. As we passed classrooms, I caught glimpses of kids twice my size sitting at individual desks organized in straight rows. Their faces were blank and bored. I decided right then and there to quit school before I ever reached sixth grade.

After what felt like days we arrived at a door covered in cartoon depictions of computer equipment. *This must be it*, I thought. The lab. All around me nervous whispers rose to a crescendo. Then our teacher swung open the door.

Inside, thirty oversized desktop computers hummed expectantly. The air was warm and thick with static. Everything smelled sterile and plastic-y, like we were smelling The Future. Our teacher told us each to pick a computer and sit down, and before she finished her sentence we were screaming and running toward the machines. Seconds later all the computers were claimed and singing to life.

We learned to type our names. I typed E R I N E R I N E R I N a hundred times until the letters filled the page and lost their meaning. At first it was fun, my fingers hopscotching across the top row to form *E R I* and then cannonballing down on the *N* key to finish it off. But soon the text spilled onto the second page and I started to come down from my computer high. In its wake was an intense but familiar pressure. A pressure in my bladder.

I had to pee. In the collective hysteria over computer lab, I didn't realize my tiny bladder was swelling to twice its normal size thanks to our snack time Juicy Juice. And now I was reaching critical capacity. I shoved my rolly chair away from the table and ran to my teacher.

"Can I go to the bathroom?" I asked, my toes tap-tapping in place.

"Do you know where the bathroom is?" she said.

I knew she was asking a legitimate question; we were far from our classroom and therefore far from the only bathroom I ever used. But I couldn't help but think things were still weird between us ever since the sand-table incident. I couldn't say no and admit that sometimes I didn't know things, and that I wasn't always right, and that maybe flooding the sand table wasn't the best idea in the history of kindergarten.

We were at an impasse: I had to choose between admitting I wasn't the smartest kid alive and getting to pee, or maintaining my dignity and holding it. So I chose option three.

"Never mind," I said. I walked over to my friend Daniel and looked over his shoulder at the repeating *D*'s *A*'s *N*'s *I*'s *E*'s *L*'s on his screen while I emptied the entire contents of my bladder onto the tiled floor behind him. It was, I had decided, the only way for me to keep my reputation.

"Erin," said my teacher, not looking up from the papers she was correcting. "Didn't you say you have to go to the bathroom?"

I glanced down at the yellow lake around my feet that was creeping outward in every direction. My classmates had started noticing. Kayla was screaming.

"Not anymore," I said.

My teacher arranged for a teacher I didn't recognize to watch over our class while she escorted me to the nurse's office. I knew things were serious because she called the replacement teacher by his first name, Peter, and apologized a lot. By the time she and I left the lab, everyone had stopped typing their names and stood around Pee Lake like they were gathering around a funeral pyre. As the door closed behind us I heard Peter telling everyone to go back to their tables, but it seemed none of my classmates could break the trance my pee held over them.

My teacher and I didn't speak once during our walk to

the nurse's office. Instead I listened to the click of her high heels echo in the empty hallway and the quiet squelching of my own sneakers. I kept wondering why she was taking me to the nurse if I wasn't sick. As far as I knew, the nurse only gave out one of two things: a Band-Aid or a DIY ice pack made from putting a couple of ice cubes into a latex glove and tying off the opening at the wrist. I wasn't sure how either of those things were going to help me un-pee my pants, but I still kind of hoped I'd get an ice pack.

When we arrived at the nurse's office it was apparent she had been expecting me. My teacher ominously explained that the nurse would "take care" of me from that point on, then left, the sound of her footsteps fading down the hall. I was alone with the nurse in her too-white office.

The nurse asked me to sit in a plastic chair by her desk, and I wondered how many pee-butts had sat there before mine. I looked at the posters that lined the walls: There were cartoon toothbrushes with faces, deodorant sticks with faces, even eyeglasses with faces. It was like some sort of hygiene-themed acid trip. I started to feel nervous looking at their unblinking expressions, but then the nurse's voice broke my concentration.

"OK, Erin, what's your family's number?" the nurse asked, picking up her desk phone.

"Three nine five," I said, swinging my heavy, wet shoes back and forth.

"Three nine five and then what?" she asked as she punched in the numbers.

"Three nine five High Street," I said.

She frowned and hung up the phone. In her top left desk drawer, she located the school's directory and flipped around until she found section *C*, and then, pulling her finger down the page, Chack. She dialed seven numbers and then waited, still frowning.

I heard a tiny electronic version of my mom's voice come through the receiver, and suddenly realized I'd have to explain to my mother why my otherwise spotless pants-peeing record had been quite literally soiled. I swung my shoes faster.

"Yes, hi, Mrs. Chack. This is Nurse Orthman calling from Oradell Public School—Yes, yes everything's fine—It's Erin—No, she had an *accident*." The nurse looked at me out of the side of her glasses.

I pretended to be interested in the ceiling tiles. Peeing my pants wasn't an accident, but I knew the nurse would shush me if I tried to explain my reasoning to her. I *had* to pee my pants so I could keep my dignity intact. Wasn't that obvious?

The nurse hung up the phone and turned toward me.

"Your mother's on her way," she explained. "Let's get you some clean pants, hm?"

She stood up and walked over to a cardboard box marked LOST AND FOUND on the side.

As soon as she yanked the cardboard flaps open I could smell the unmistakable scent of Other People's Clothes. The nurse dug around the box until she found something that looked my size.

"How about these?" she asked, holding the pair up to her chest. They were sweatpants, heather gray and elastic at the ankles. I couldn't tell if they once belonged to a boy or a girl. And even more concerning, I couldn't tell why the boy or the girl no longer needed the pants. What happened to him or her and why wasn't he or she wearing pants?

"No, thank you," I said.

"I'm sure you'd be much more comfortable in dry pants," she said. She shook the sweatpants back and forth in front of her, trying to sell me on them with her presentation.

"I'm fine," I said.

The nurse balled up the pants and threw them back in the box.

"Well, do you want to use the bathroom?" she asked.

I was certain I had never needed a bathroom less in my life, having just left half my body weight in fluids on the computer lab floor.

"No," I said.

She let out a long sigh. "Well then. Let's just wait for your mom."

I stayed quiet for a second while trying to avoid eye contact with the smiling bar of soap on the wall.

"Can I have an ice pack?" I asked.

My mom showed up a few minutes later looking harried and slightly out of breath. Apologizing to no one in particular, she ran over to me and squeezed my top half against her hip while I was still seated in the chair. I wrapped my arms around her thigh, relief spreading through my entire body.

"What happened, Er?" she asked.

"I didn't know where the bathroom was," I said. I didn't feel like I had to explain about the sand table and the tank tops and the back of the carpet at circle time—she'd understand. But before I knew it I was crying. I wiped my hot, wet tears on the leg of her overalls while she rubbed my back in big circles with her open palm.

When I had calmed down, my mom brought me into the nurse's bathroom and helped me change into fresh clothes—including pants with a definitive backstory that didn't involve missing children—that she had brought from home. She plopped my wet ones in a ShopRite bag, washed her hands, turned to me, and asked if I was ready to go home. Seconds later I was skipping across the front lawn of the school toward our big gray van, feeling pounds lighter without the soggy weight of my pee pants. It was spring and I didn't need a jacket. The dogwood trees that lined the sidewalk exploded with fat, white blossoms. *It's so easy to leave school early*, I thought. *Just a little pee and you're free.* I'd have to remember that for the next time I wanted to spend the day watching cartoons with my cat.

Back at our house, my mom peeled off my leggings and put me in the tub while warm soapy water filled up around me. I scooped a handful of bubbles and patted them onto my cheeks to form a tickly beard. I was happy to be home.

Sitting on the bathroom floor next to the tub, my mom dangled her arm over the edge so that her fingertips kissed the surface of the water. She rested her head on her shoulder and looked at me sideways.

"Do I have to go back to school?" I asked, adding more bubbles to my beard.

"No, you've had enough school today, I think," she said, drawing her now wet hand under her chin so she could look at me right side up. I looked at her looking at me.

"What?" I said.

"You know, I peed my pants once in school, too," she said.

"You did?" I asked, trying to imagine my full-sized mother in a kid-sized body.

"Mhm," she said, "I was sitting at my desk raising my hand to ask if I could go to the bathroom, but the nun didn't see me. So I started waving my hand all around, hoping that would get her attention. And when I stretched too far forward I started peeing right there at my desk."

"How old were you?" I asked.

"Second grade," she said.

I had seen second graders on the playground during recess. They were tall and loud and practically full-grown adults. A child doing a childish thing is one thing, but an almost-adult child doing a childish thing is full-on social suicide.

"Oh," I said, pretending not to judge. "Were you embarrassed?"

"Yes," she said. "Were you?"

"No," I said, keeping my eyes glued to the pile of bubbles in my cupped hands. "I wanted to do it. So that I didn't have to tell Ms. Mele that I didn't know where the bathroom was, remember?"

"Right," she said, dumping a cupful of water on my head and washing away my bubble beard. "My mistake."

About two years later, when I was in second grade, I accidentally peed in my best friend Katie's walk-in closet. I had spent the night at her house, like I did most Fridays, but refused to use the bathroom because her mom's boyfriend, Angelo, was in the house. I was just so sure that he would absolutely accidentally walk in on me, as if the concepts of locks and knocking had never been invented on Katie's side of the street. I decided to wait until after Angelo was gone, but the problem was that he also spent the night. From six in the evening until the morning when we woke up, all the Kool-Aid and ice pops and soda we had consumed filtered into my bladder with no way to escape.

The next day while I was changing from my pajama pants to my jeans, the air hitting my naked bottom half tricked my brain into thinking I was hovering over a toilet. Before I could stop it, twelve hours of piss was ricocheting off the thick gray carpet of Katie's closet, splashing my discarded pajama pants and her many pairs of shoes lined up in a neat row against the baseboard. It hadn't been a thought-out decision or an act of defiance. It was a complete and total accident, a Grade-A Baby move.

I don't count that one, though. You can't technically pee your pants if you're not wearing any.

MEMENTO MORI

I didn't party my entire first year of college, but it wasn't for lack of trying. My roommate, Olivia, and I attempted to go to a total of three parties before giving up on the idea and spending our subsequent Friday nights taking the T to every single frozen yogurt shop in the city of Boston. I don't even like frozen yogurt that much.

The first party we tried to attend happened our orientation weekend at Boston University. A girl in our program said she'd seen a flier on the telephone poles near MIT for a "Chocolate Party" and was thinking of going. Olivia and I decided we'd tag along. Drinking beer and eating chocolate with other people who also like drinking beer and eating chocolate sounded like a wild time, and we, two fun and cool college freshmen, were down for it. We ended up walking from BU to MIT with a group of no less than fifteen other girls, which is a journey that can either take forty minutes in sensible shoes or upward of an hour with our particular caravan. Finally, we arrived at the address listed on the flier, bloodied and blistered, and knocked on the door. A guy a few years older than us opened the door, and inside we could hear the unmistakable sounds of a dance party.

The guy surveyed our fifteen-person mob of freshmen girls. He sucked air through his teeth, the way you might if you saw a toddler who was running too fast trip and fall on the ground.

"Did you guys think this was a party with free chocolate?" he asked.

"Were we supposed to bring our own?" asked Courtnee, the captain of our cross-river procession.

As the guy patiently explained, the party was a mixer for all the Black student groups in the area to meet one another. Our mob let out a collective "Ohhh." That made a lot more sense than eating chocolate with strangers.

The guy apologized, and we apologized even more, a fifteen-person sorry party. Then we turned and left, stopping at a convenience store along the way home. We were still in the mood for chocolate.

Once classes began, Olivia heard about a frat party from a girl in her Spanish class. We decided the words "frat party" could not be misinterpreted, and anyway, the frats were on our side of the river, a brisk fifteen-minute walk down Bay State Road.

That night Olivia and I selected deliberately casual outfits and shoes with extra cushioning. We set out from our dorms with only a handful of girls and arrived at a brownstone on the outskirts of campus a short while later.

A guy in a backward baseball cap stopped us before we could walk up the stoop.

"You guys look like you're eighteen," he said.

"We are eighteen!" I said, like maybe the party was in short supply of that exact demographic.

"Guys, it's the first week of school," he said, rubbing the bridge of his nose, like he was tired of explaining this concept to freshmen infants. "We have to at least *pretend* like we're not letting minors in."

"We're eighteen days away from being twenty-two," I said. "We're quintuplets."

"Nice try."

The frat bro told us to leave and come back when we were legal. I responded by pretending to vomit into my cupped hands.

The last party lead came to me in the dining hall. I was pouring cereal into a gallon-sized Ziploc bag when a shadow descended on me. I looked up to find a nine-foot hockey player standing next to me, his head eclipsing the light.

"Hey," I said, since we'd made eye contact.

"Hey," he said. "You live in this building?"

I tried not to audibly gag at the college version of "You come here often?"

"Yeah," I said, shaking my sack of cereal down and pinching it closed. "Do you?"

"Yeah," he said. I wondered if they had to special order a bed for his treelike body, or if he pushed his desk up against the end for extra legroom. "There's a hockey party at the Dugout tonight. You should come. And bring friends."

I raised an eyebrow. "Maybe I will," I said.

"Then maybe I'll see you there then," he said.

I tucked my cereal bag under my arm and wished him a pleasant afternoon. An hour later, Olivia and I paced around our dorm room trying to suss out if this was a real lead or another dead end.

"First of all, he *invited* you, so the odds of us getting turned away this time are very low," she said, tapping a pen on her chin. I sat on my desk chair A. C. Slater–style and watched her pace in the small space between our twin beds.

"Unless he's a sociopath and he did it as a joke, like a rich kid in an eighties movie."

"It's unlikely, but I'm not ruling it out," she said.

"Isn't the Dugout a bar? How are we going to get into a bar?"

"It can't be a *bar* bar—he knows you live in Towers! This is a freshman, *maybe* sophomore dorm."

"Aren't athletes all, like, thirty-five years old? Maybe he thought I was also an athlete, and therefore also thirty-five years old."

"I don't think he thought that," Olivia said, stopping in front of me.

"Oh, you don't think I could be a college-level athlete?"

"I don't think you look thirty-five!"

"Aw, that's so sweet," I said.

It went on like this until the sun started to set and we decided the only way to find out if this was a real party was to go. It took us an entire hour to get dressed, both of us trying to nail a look that said, "This is definitely not our first college party, ha ha ha, not even close." Before we left we took a photo together on my laptop to commemorate the event and preserve our pre-party glow. We knew everything would be different when we returned in the small hours of night, tired and buzzing from our first college party as we crawled into our beds.

Less than five minutes later Olivia and I strode confidently up to the Dugout, which was a basement bar we had walked past countless times but had never gone inside. I squeezed her arm as we approached and mouthed an unnecessary, "It's go time."

A large man wearing all black was seated in a chair outside the front door. I prayed he was there to wish us a happy alcohol time and maybe stamp our hands with a smiley face for good measure.

"Are you checking IDs?" I asked.

"No, I'm suntanning," he said, pointing at the moon.

I reached into my bag and handed him my portrait-oriented ID that proclaimed in red block text that I was an eighteen-year-old child who couldn't legally drink. Perhaps my confidence would throw him off, or he'd feel really, really bad for how hard I was trying and let us in anyway.

"This ID says you're eighteen," he said.

"That is correct," I said.

"This is a bar," he said.

"Yes, sir," I said.

He handed me my ID back. "You can't come into this bar if you're eighteen."

"That sounds about right," I said, spinning on my heel and hooking Olivia's arm before the hockey player could glance out the window and witness the most embarrassing moment of my entire life.

We slunk back to our dorm and spent the evening watching *South Park* on our couch and passing a pint of Ben & Jerry's between us before falling asleep at 11:30 p.m.

I stopped trying to go to parties after that. It only made me feel desperate and uncool, and I figured I could feel desperate and uncool on my own and without having to walk so far. I spent my free time skating *a lot*, usually alone and in straight lines down the Charles River Esplanade until my legs turned to jelly from the rumbling of the asphalt. I went for a lot of runs. I visited every museum in the Boston area, twice. I made weird, experimental horror films with my friends based on premises like "What if the Easter Bunny were a murderer?" and "What if *everyone* were murderers?"

In the end, the most illegal fun we had that year was when Olivia went home to visit her mom in Connecticut and swiped a bottle of merlot off the wine rack on her way out. We drank the wine from plastic cups in our dorm room with two other girls, leaving us each with the amount of alcohol most Italian children drink with dinner.

During what should have been my sophomore year, while I was home sick with cancer, I discovered from Facebook that Olivia had figured out how to go to parties. I clicked through albums showing her clutching red cups with her polished fingers, her head tossed back to reveal the most beautiful angles of her face, her eyes half-closed in fuzzy merriment. I rubbed my hand over my naked scalp and felt a twinge of sadness. The closest I had gotten to a party since being home was when a chemo nurse slipped a sleeve of small plastic pill cups into my backpack and told me, "Do shots with these, but only when you're better."

When I returned to school in January later that year, Olivia had left Boston to study abroad in Madrid, where the wine was "cheaper than water," she scrawled on a postcard, and the legal drinking age was eighteen. A lot of my first-year floor mates had dispersed to random parts of campus or different schools entirely, leaving me to start over, socially speaking. It was like freshman year all over again, except now I had no hair and no friends and everyone else had plenty of both.

So when a girl in my Newswriting and Reporting lecture called out to me after our second night of class, I did my best not to scare her away, the way you might keep your movements slow and steady around a baby deer.

"Hey, so, why are you in this class in the spring? Most journalism students take it in the fall," she asked.

"Yeah, I wasn't here last semester because I had sick. I mean I had cancer. I wasn't here last semester because I had cancer." I immediately wanted to melt into the sewer grates.

"Oh shit," she said, her Midwestern accent saturating every word. "I switched majors. Your excuse is better."

We both lived in South Campus, and for some reason, even after that exchange, she offered to walk with me there. I learned her name was Carroll, she was from Chicago, and she still wasn't sure if she wanted to study journalism. I mostly nodded a lot as she talked, not wanting to repeat the "I had sick" moment. After we crossed the bridge over I-90 to the brownstone village that makes up South Campus, Carroll stopped short at the steps of a garden apartment.

"Oh! This is Robert and Fernando's place. Do you know Robert and Fernando?" she asked.

"Um, am I supposed to?" I asked. I briefly wondered if Robert and Fernando were perhaps a team of juggling squirrels, a South Campus street performing act that everyone but me knew about.

"No, it's just that every time I try to introduce someone to Robert and Fernando they're like 'Oh my god! I love Robert and Fernando!' They're such fun guys."

Without waiting for a response she walked down the steps to knock on the door. A moment later, a tall, lanky boy answered. His un-gelled Mohawk flopped over to one side like the fin of an orca raised in captivity. His red eyes brimmed with tears.

"Oh my god! Robert, what's wrong?" Carroll asked.

"Alex broke up with me." Robert wiped his nose on the sleeve of his thermal shirt, leaving a snail trail of snot on the dark blue fabric.

"Oh nooo," Carroll cooed, and they hugged. He sniffled into her hair as she made sad shushing sounds, and they rocked back and forth like they were slow dancing to music I couldn't hear.

This Robert dude seemed fun in a universe where funerals are an ideal Saturday night out. The awkward feeling in my gut intensified.

"Uh, I'm Erin," I said, waving from five feet away.

Robert lifted his head out of Carroll's hair and looked at me as if I'd just materialized in front of them.

"Hiii," he said, untangling himself from Carroll and pulling me into a new, fresh hug. "It's so nice to meet you. I'm Robert Pearson Roche III."

I patted him on the back more out of surprise than con-
solation. "I'm Erin . . . Chack," I muffled into his shoulder. As
soon as we peeled apart, Carroll launched into making plans.

"Listen, Robert, we've got to do a dinner party tonight."

Robert crossed his arms and nodded his head in
agreement.

"OK," he said. "Why?"

Carroll smacked his arm. "Because! You need to get
over Alex, Erin needs to meet Fernando, and I want to
introduce all three of you to Julian."

"Oh shit, you're right," Robert said, as if her suggestion
was as obvious as telling someone with a fork in their eye
that they should go to the hospital.

They made plans for eight, and volunteered Fernando—
without his consent—to make his famous coconut curry.
When everything was set they turned and faced me together.

"Does that work for you?" Carroll asked.

"I—uh." I looked back and forth between their faces,
Carroll's brown eyes shining beneath a neat line of brunette
bangs and Robert's cheeks still slick with tears. I was origi-
nally planning on grabbing dinner alone at the dining hall
and then maybe getting a jump on our first assignment for
Newswriting after that. But as they waited for my answer
with expectant smiles, I suddenly felt it would be rude to

refuse the plans two near-strangers constructed out of thin air in less time than it takes to brush one's teeth.

"Sure," I said. "I'm free as a bird."

As I got ready that night, I ran through our interaction in my head and tried to pinpoint the exact moment I went from complete stranger to necessary dinner party guest. I never quite figured it out.

At 8:07 I left my dorm and wondered if I was supposed to bring something, like wine, and then wondered where I was supposed to get wine, not being of legal drinking age. At 8:09 I arrived—the apartment was only two streets away from my dorm—empty-handed. I stood outside and asked myself what I was doing there. I knocked before I could figure out the answer.

A man who was not Robert answered.

"Hi," I said. "Fernando?"

"Yesss, hiii," Fernando said, immediately hugging me. He was a few inches shorter than me, which made him a lot of inches shorter than Robert. I felt relieved he wasn't crying.

Fernando pulled me by the wrist into the apartment, a basement studio with two beds, two desks, and one couch. Red scarves cloaked the lamps, which gave the room the illusion of a brothel that also happened to be covered in college-level textbooks and superhero posters. The scent of lit candles competed with the smell of simmering coconut curry. The air felt thick, like a bathroom after taking a shower.

"Is that Erin?" Robert's voice sang from the alcoved kitchen. When he appeared around the corner he looked different, mainly because he had stopped crying and his Mohawk had been gelled erect. He crossed the room to hug me, hands still shod in oven mitts, and I wondered if this was what it was like to be in the family from *Full House*.

"Is Carroll here?" I asked, like she might be crouching under one of the semi-lofted beds.

"She's on her way," Robert sang, again, and made his way back to the kitchen.

"And she's bringing Julian," Fernando said, wiggling his eyebrows.

"Right. Who's Julian?" I asked.

"A boy she thinks she likes and she wants to see if we like him, too," Fernando explained. "Ugh, I hope we like him. Carroll's *the best*. Isn't Carroll the best?"

"I . . . think so," I said, replaying the entirety of our fifteen-minute relationship in my head.

"I have to tell you something," Fernando said.

"What?" I said, cautiously. What could he possibly have to tell me besides the location of the bathroom?

"I love your hair. It's absolutely gorgeous," he said.

"Oh, god. Thank you," I said, reaching up to touch my crop of short, new hair. Before I'd left my dorm I'd mussed it up with some pomade I'd swiped from home. It was finally starting to feel like my hair again. Hair that belonged to me.

"Doesn't she look like Alek Wek?" Robert called from the kitchen.

"Yes!" Fernando agreed.

"What is alickwek?" I asked.

Before I got an answer, Carroll and Julian let themselves into the apartment.

We ate dinner sitting cross-legged on the ground in front of the couch. Somehow, despite the fact that they were a few months younger than I was, Robert and Fernando had an endless supply of screw-top wine. We made it through two bottles by the time dinner was over. I lay back on the carpet, tummy full and eyes bleary, to listen to Carroll sing softly to herself, Robert keep a beat on his knee, and Fernando and Julian discuss Catholicism's place in modern society.

I couldn't have known then that one day, in the not-so-distant future, I would sign a lease with Robert. We would live together with Olivia and his friend Charles in a party house in Allston. We would throw too many keggers and spend whole Sundays cleaning up after them. I would lose my favorite photograph of him and my best friend, Alijah, in their bathing suits in the bathtub. We would start a tradition called Gin and Tonic Tuesdays and write papers with one eye closed. We would spend a Valentine's Day together eating heart-shaped meatballs and talking about our One True Loves. Sean, mine, and Alex, his. We would graduate and move out. He would get back together with Alex. They would live happily ever after.

I would eventually move to New York. Carroll would, too. She would start dating women, and I would understand the significance of the time she readjusted my blouse and kissed me hard on the mouth on my twenty-first birthday. We would not see each other often despite living so close, but I would always feel connected to her, since so much of my college career was spent trying to figure out our respective futures on long walks near the Charles River or lying on the floor of her apartment or sitting on chilly porches while parties raged on inside.

Fernando and I would share recipes and thoughts on God and, one night in particular, an entire bottle of absinthe. But after college we would eventually lose touch and become the type of friends to make ambitious plans to see each other whenever we happened to be in the same city for work stuff. On the cab rides back to my hotel after our plans inevitably fell through, I would kick myself for not making more of an effort with one of the nicest people I would ever know.

As for Julian, I would never see him again, since Carroll would proclaim the next morning during a hungover breakfast (the first of many) at the dining hall that she didn't feel a connection. And we would all shrug and tuck into our mountain of scrambled eggs, not thinking much of it.

But that night, Carroll, Robert, and Fernando were all still strangers, strangers with free food, but strangers nonetheless. While they talked and hummed and drummed on I tried to figure out how I made it to here. Not just to Robert and Fernando's humid, red-tinted apartment, but to Boston, to college, to the other side of cancer. The harder I tried to figure it out the more my thoughts blurred together, and I let them, enjoying the giddiness from cheap wine and the thrill of not knowing what was coming next.

When there was a lull in the conversation, I sat up on my elbows and nodded toward the couch where Fernando and Julian were sitting.

"Julian, what's that tattoo?" I asked, my head a little dizzy from the sudden movement.

Without hesitation, Julian stood up on the couch and pulled his shirt collar down to reveal the curly letters inked on his chest. For a second I thought he'd misheard me and was going to recite the Pledge of Allegiance, and I'd already decided I was too embarrassed to correct him.

"MEMENTO MORI," he yelled, and everyone watched, quietly, respectfully, as he launched into a performance. "Re-MEM-ber that you HAVE . . . to *die*."

It was a slam poem, one he had memorized and evidently prepared to perform for us. As he yell-recited each line, I checked the others' faces for a hint of irony or concealed judgment. I found none. This, it seemed, was a normal reaction to someone inquiring about a tattoo in the Robert-Fernando home. Theirs was a sanctuary of the offbeat, the outcasted. All were welcome, whether it be a woman with a shaved head or a man with a morbid tattoo.

Of course, I thought. Of course I finally get to go to a party—yes a *dinner* party, but still technically a party—and I end up in a poetry dungeon listening to a stranger yell un-rhyming lines about death with increasing urgency. And yet, a not-so-small part of me knew this was exactly where I was meant to be. Julian and I weren't so different. We were both death-obsessed and screaming (though one of us chose to do so internally). His tattoo, like my short hair, was a constant reminder of what could have been and what will one day be. Somehow I'd ended up in a room of people who nodded along to Julian's poem instead of snickering, as I might have done one year earlier. This would not be the last night I spent lying on this carpet, in this red room, with these people, I realized, and I instantly felt the subtle, in-audible click of things falling into place deep inside my gut.

When Julian finished his poem, everyone clapped their hands around their wine glasses while he hopped down off the couch. Once he was seated back on the floor he turned toward me as if nothing had happened.

"So," he said. "You got any tattoos?"

ACKNOWLEDGMENTS

This is my first book, so buckle up, 'cause I've got a lot of people to thank.

First, I must grovel at the feet of my editor, Tiffany Liao, who floated down from heaven in the form of an email one July morning asking, "Hey, have you ever thought about writing a book?" Tiff, look at me—LOOK ME IN THE EYES—you single-handedly made my lifelong dream come true and I will think of you on my deathbed.

And I bow down to my agent, Tina Wexler, who I knew was my agent when I made a joke about giving birth to a book the first time we met and you, T, warned me to watch out for the corners. Thank you for taking a chance on me and for not kicking me out for starting every email with "Wtf is happening rn . . ."

Thank you to my publicist, Elyse Marshall, for being my publicist and for being from New Jersey. I am so humbled that you believe in this project and I hope we (me and this book) make you proud! Let's get our second holes pierced together at the Paramus Park Mall.

I am grateful to my copy editor, Samantha Hoback, and my proofreaders, Jeff Somoya and Kate Frentzel, who had to make decisions over words like Fudgsicle (the ice pop) and fudgesicle (something you should never, ever look up on Urban Dictionary). Thank you and also sorry.

I am forever indebted to my Razorbill family, especially our daddy Ben Schrank. I wrote that to make you uncomfortable. Did it work?

So much love and thanks to my BuzzFeed family, a circus of misfits who gave me a home. Thank you especially to Eugene Ventimiglia for being the one to extend a hand.

And to my actual family, the Chack Pack, the GREATEST family to ever live, thank you the most. Dad, thank you for reading to me every night. Mom, thank you for being my biggest (and only) fan. Liz, thank you for sending cards when you knew I needed them. Emily, thank you for always being a text away. And our cat Ashes, thank you for staying alive for nineteen years even though I'm sure you have better things to do. I love you all very much.

I am grateful for all my teachers but specifically these ones: Mrs. Helmis, Mrs. Carney, Ms. Milch, and Professor Burak. Thanks for knowing this could one day happen even though every time you told me I was like, "Lol, yeah right."

And many thanks to my college writing group: Alijah Marie "My Best Girl" Case, Jackson Tobin, Professor Antonio Elefano, and the bartender at the Dugout. Also sorry, Antonio, for calling you on the verge of tears multiple times over the past two years even though you had a brand-new baby who was also always on the verge of tears.

Thank you to Jasmine Lywen-Dill, who I know is scanning this page looking for her name. You found it!

To all the families who opened their homes as writing retreats for me, holy shit! Thank you! I got to pretend I was Hemingway, but with a much shorter beard. For their upstate house, thank you to the Stasi family. For their Cape house, thank you to the Macfarlane family. For their chicken coop, thank you to the Rankel and Flister family.

Thank you to Craig Moskowitz for saving my life. Thank you to Kimarie Knowles for saving my brain. Thank you to every single person who works at Memorial Sloan-Kettering Cancer Center. Thank you to all the families; the borough of Oradell; and my favorite band, Nada Surf, for supporting my family when my mom and I were sick.

Thank you to Roald Dahl, Five Corners Deli, the New Oxford American Dictionary, Guinness, feminism, and sleeping eight hours every night.

Thank you to YOU, the person holding this book. I can't believe you're real, and I super, super owe you one.

And finally, to Sean, oh my god, thank you for staying quiet for two long years while I wrote this book in our apartment. Thank you for not breaking up with me whenever I shushed you for clinking a glass too loud. Thank you for all the great advice on art and fear. Thank you for the long walks and the long talks and for knowing me so well. Thank you for giving me space and for staying so close. Thank you for letting me tell our story. Thank you for loving me. And thank you for reading this far, because I know you hate reading. I love you, Sarge!